I0889940

FIRST AID for YOUR Ministry

SUPPORTING THOSE WHO MINISTER

Edward E. Moody Jr., Ph.D.

randall house

First Aid for Those Who Minister

Published by Randall House
114 Bush Road
Nashville, TN 37217
Visit www.randallhouse.com

13-ISBN 9780892654123

Printed in the United States of America

FIRST AID FOR THOSE WHO MINISTER

> *The saying is trustworthy: If anyone aspires to the office of overseer, he desires a noble task.*
>
> 1 Timothy 3:1

There is nothing like ministry. Nothing is as exciting as experiencing life with people in a congregation or as exhausting as helping people through the inevitable difficulties that arise across the lifespan. Nothing is as rewarding as watching families grow over time or more disconcerting than lacking time for your own development or family. Nothing is more exhilarating than seeing the lives of others changed, or more disappointing than seeing a person slide away from their faith. Nothing is more fulfilling than working alongside others or more painful than feeling the sting of criticism or even betrayal from someone with whom you have worked closely. Nothing is like the sense of community felt as you enjoy fellowship in the ministry or like the loneliness you feel when you think no one understands what you are experiencing. Nothing is like the fulfilling feeling one has when they have ministered well, and nothing is like the despair felt after erring in ministry by failing in some way or letting others down. Nothing is more important than ministry, but no one experiences more self-doubt or feels less appreciated than those who minister. There is nothing like the highs and lows of the ministry. This book is for those who do this important work.

You Might Benefit From First Aid If . . .

You feel like you can never catch up with everything you need to do

You have begun to dislike your work

You often struggle to sleep as you worry about the church

Your family feels like they live in a fishbowl

You wonder if your ministry efforts have been in vain

Someone says they need to speak to you and your initial response is dread

You feel like you have no one with whom you can talk

You feel like your efforts are unappreciated

You feel like no one understands you

You feel you are inadequate to minister

You feel like you could be more effective

Ministry is Difficult Everywhere and in Every Context

Several years ago, I was enjoying a quiet evening in a country far from home after spending the day teaching. A minister in that country came into the home where I was resting and began to discuss some of the struggles pastors were experiencing. He described the stress, disappointment, feelings of loneliness and inadequacy associated with pastoring. He said in some cases the children of ministers were not interested in going into the ministry because of the difficulties they had observed. I sensed he thought these problems were unique to his country. The more we talked, the more I realized the commonality of ministry problems. I have been with pastors from diverse church sizes, different denominations, and in different settings. It seems from time to time that everyone who ministers wonders if some of their experiences are unique to them. However, my own observations, research on pastors, and the Bible indicate that the problems of ministry are not confined to a specific country, a particular denomination, or a certain historical period. Ministry is difficult everywhere.

The ministry has always been difficult. Throughout the Bible, we see those who minister dealing with difficulty. Moses faced constant complaining and criticism (Numbers 11–17). Elijah dealt with threats (1 Kings 19:2), disappointment (1 Kings 19:4), and loneliness (1 Kings 19:10, 14). Jeremiah felt like a failure and was attacked by his own people (Jeremiah 20:2). John the Baptist battled disillusionment (Matthew 11:2-3), perhaps thinking his ministry efforts had been in vain. Peter failed, always speaking before thinking something through (Luke 9:33) and letting down those he cared for the most (Luke 22:54-62). Paul made no secret of his constant suffering (2 Corinthians 11:16-33). Even Jesus knew the pain, stress, and loneliness of the ministry (Luke 22:44).

Ministry Is Difficult in Many Ways

Ministry = Stress

Ministry = Disappointment

Ministry = Loneliness

Ministry = Enduring Complaining and Criticism

So let us begin by admitting the many challenges faced in the ministry. I too have experienced this. Most people would assume that working in a correctional setting is stressful. It just so happens that on my first day of work as a pastor, I began that day working in a correctional facility. As I walked out of the facility after working with a group of sex offenders, I remember thinking, "Now I get to work with normal people in a fulfilling environment." I thought the ministry would be less difficult. I quickly discerned that the challenges of ministry were more pervasive than my former work.

In many ways, one cannot truly understand or anticipate the difficulty of the ministry until they are in it. I remember driving on Interstate 40 going through Raleigh, North Carolina when I sensed this. I thought, "Pastoring a church is going to be harder than I thought." As I looked back on my life just a few weeks before I began to pastor, I realized how it had changed in ways I had not anticipated. For just a moment, I thought the easiest thing for me to do would be to quit the ministry and go back to that life.

Even as I considered the difficulty of the ministry, I experienced the strong draw or call of the ministry. I was already beginning to sense that I was part of something far more important and rewarding than I could have understood before entering the ministry. Today, I could not imagine quitting. The research indicates that many pastors who persevere in the ministry feel that way. One study has indicated that two-thirds of pastors said they were even more confident of their call to the ministry than they were when they began.[1] If you will stick with the ministry, your sense of call will probably increase rather than decrease.

How then will they call on him in whom they have not believed? And how are they to believe in him of whom they have never heard? And how are they to hear without someone preaching? And how are they to preach unless they are sent? As it is written, "How beautiful are the feet of those who preach the good news!"

Romans 10:14-15

Over time the value of ministry often becomes more evident. Paul described the importance of preachers of the gospel when he quoted Isaiah 52:7 and Nahum 1:15 in his letter to the Romans. He described the beautiful feet of those who bring this good news. All faithful Christians perform this function on some level. However, as a pastor you spend much of your time taking the good news to people in the midst of all sorts of difficulty. Even though most of us do not think of our feet as being particularly attractive, Paul says they are beautiful because of the good news they carry.

So much is lost when a minister leaves the ministry. In a practical way, their expertise is not easily replaced. When a minister stumbles and falls, the church they pastored or the ministry they led is damaged far more than it would have been had it been a secular enterprise. Ministers play an important role in the lives of others. Therefore, we will identify some of the major threats to those who do ministry.

What Challenges Do Ministers Face?

Each minister and ministry are different but there are many situations and common concerns faced by all who minister on some level. A few years ago, I asked some ministers about the barriers they experienced in the ministry. They reported many challenges, but the top barriers were disappointment (43%), conflict (34%), time constraints (29%), inadequate preparation (26%), depression (26%), and sexual temptation (22%).[2] We will examine these major concerns, and describe activities ministers can engage in to protect themselves and to enable them to be good stewards of their ministry. We will explore the lives of biblical characters and review research studies on these challenges. The Scripture speaks directly to the struggles of the ministry. Passages on the qualifications and characteristics that those who minister must possess (Titus 1; 1 Timothy 3; 1 Peter 5) are the antidotes to the specific challenges faced in ministry. My desire is for ministers to be as effective and fulfilled as they can be. There is nothing like ministry, so it is important that we harness the opportunity to be a good steward of the time we have to engage in this noble task.

To what degree do you have the following?

Too much to do and not enough time to do it

←---→

Rarely — Very Frequently

A sense of being under constant pressure

←---→

Rarely — Very Frequently

No time to relax and refresh

←---→

Rarely — Very Frequently

Personal or family plans that are often canceled or interrupted

←---→

Rarely — Very Frequently

Expectations to meet needs for which you lack resources and expertise

←---→

Rarely — Very Frequently

Threats to Ministers: Stress

Stress is a major threat to pastors. Every day there is someone who is sick, dying, straying from the path, or slightly disgruntled in need of tender loving pastoral care. On the previous page are some items from the work of Berry et al. and Lee and Iverson-Gilbert.[3] These are some of the situations that result in stress in the ministry. What are some of the ways you are experiencing stress? Is stress sapping the energy out of your life and ministry?

> *I came that they may have life and have it abundantly.*
>
> John 10:10b

Have you ever preached from John 10:10 about the abundant life found in Christ and felt a bit like a hypocrite? It may seem as though you can never really get away from the stress of the ministry. At times I have said to myself, "There will not be that abundant life today but maybe tomorrow." Most pastors have watched over an ill church member and felt their heart sink as they realized the person was unlikely to survive. You begin to feel exhausted as you realize the person will likely die while you are in the midst of a much needed vacation or highly anticipated trip. A time of anticipated refreshment and renewal can turn into a period of concern, stress, and heartbreak.

Then there are the times when one really does feel like they are living the abundant life only to learn of a tragic event experienced by someone or a brewing conflict in the congregation, thrusting one back into a very stressful period of ministry. The stress can go on for days, weeks, and even months.

There can even be stress as you go about the community. Someone has an accident; a neighbor dies suddenly and you find yourself trying to help someone on the worst day of their life. One cannot help but feel stress.

> "It's not the things in ministry that kill you, it's the things you don't get done. Every night you leave you know that there's another twelve people you should call, another three books you should read, another eight people you need to visit in the hospital."

Too Much to Do

There is so much important work to do, as the pastor quoted previously indicated.[4] There are sermons to prepare, Bible studies to outline, people to disciple, leaders to train, pre-marital counseling (and post-marital too), funerals to preach, programs to plan, not to mention strategic planning and vision casting. It seems like no matter what you do, how much you work, you can never really catch up.

I suppose you could work every hour of a day and still fail to get all the work of the ministry done. The data indicate that pastors work a lot. In one old study that looked at ministers from different denominations, they found that Lutherans reported working 48 hours a week, while Methodists and Episcopalians reported 52.[5]

The stress of the work is often compounded as one begins to realize they often lack the expertise or resources needed to address an issue or situation.[6] We need expertise in almost everything: counseling, health care, affordable housing, debt reduction techniques, family law, and so much more. The minister knows high intensity living too well.

How is a pastor to cope? Some pastors cut all non-ministry activities out of their life, including time for the spiritual disciplines, time with their family, and time for themselves. Rather than improving, problems begin to multiply. Consider the comments of a pastor's wife below about high intensity living from a study of clergy families.[7]

> "He has a different schedule . . . he has no personal time. Any time he can be called—it's like he is on call . . . we have a plan to go somewhere then suddenly there's a need to adjust the schedule because there's a conflict ."

Could your spouse make the same statement about you? If one continues on this path, resentment in the family can begin to build as seen below.[8]

> "Sometimes he has no more time for us . . . I say, 'Why is it that you don't have time for us? But when it comes to others, you immediately tend to them even if we need you?'"

High intensity living is not a new problem in the ministry. Consider the example of Moses (Exodus 18) as he ministered to the Israelites. He was doing important work, but his days began early and ended late, and they were filled with difficult people problems (Exodus 18:13). I wonder if Moses ever felt like he lacked the resources and expertise to do what needed to be done. He definitely felt overwhelmed as he described below.

> *How can I bear by myself the weight and burden of you and your strife?*
>
> Deuteronomy 1:12

It sounds like Moses was in a spiral of too much to do with too few resources and that he was too tired to find a way out. Zipporah may have often said, "Why is it that you don't have time for us?"

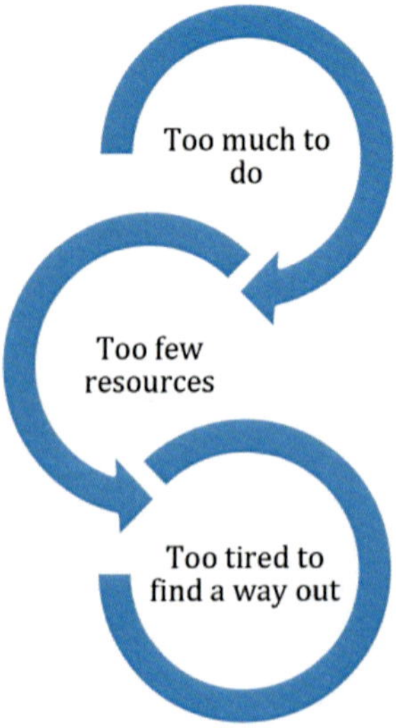

Jethro provided some important advice to his son-in-law (which we will look at later) and pointed out that this lifestyle was not good for Moses or his people (Exodus 18:17-18). What if Jethro came to your church and your home? What might he see and what might he say?

How often do you find yourself engaged in . . .

Ongoing high-intensity living—running from one place to the next

←---→

Rarely — Very Frequently

Doing too much is bad for us, our family, and our ministry. Jesus also knew this feeling. Consider the events recorded in Matthew 9. Jesus came by boat to His own city (Matthew 9:1). He healed a man who was paralyzed (Matthew 9:2) and was immediately criticized (Matthew 9:3). He called and began discipling Matthew (Matthew 9:9), and taught a lesson on mercy (Matthew 9:13). He answered hostile questions about fasting (Matthew 9:14). He was asked to raise a girl from the dead (Matthew 9:18), but was sidetracked by a woman in need of help for a problem she had struggled with for many years (Matthew 9:22). Eventually, He raised the girl from the dead (Matthew 9:25). Later He healed two blind men (Matthew 9:30), cast a demon out of another (Matthew 9:33), and faced more criticism (Matthew 9:34). Jesus knew what it felt like to have too much to do. No wonder the chapter ends with Him asking that the disciples pray for more workers (Matthew 9:38).

Most people in churches are unaware of the stress they place upon their pastor. Then again, it may be best they are unaware because the stress is usually unavoidable. Parishioners cannot control when they get sick, have an accident, die, or have a wayward child or a marital problem. They are usually unaware that when they are in crisis, several others in the congregation are as well. To do ministry is to do life with a congregation. Their pain is your pain (Romans 12:15); their stress is your stress. We must learn how to effectively cope with and even use stress positively lest it endanger us, our family, and our ministry. Consider some of the questions adapted from the work of Berry et al. and Lee and Iverson-Gilbert.[9]

Is this you?

I am often asked to perform a ministry task at the last minute

←--→

Rarely Very Frequently

My sleep is often interrupted by a phone call from a member regarding an unimportant issue

←--→

Rarely Very Frequently

I frequently deal with blurred boundaries/role conflict/issues I should not be expected to handle

←--→

Rarely Very Frequently

I deal with situations where no matter what I do, many people will be dissatisfied

←--→

Rarely Very Frequently

Now in these days when the disciples were increasing in number, a complaint by the Hellenists arose against the Hebrews because their widows were being neglected in the daily distribution. And the twelve summoned the full number of the disciples and said, "It is not right that we should give up preaching the word of God to serve tables.

Acts 6:1-2

Unrealistic Expectations

Another source of stress in the ministry is unrealistic expectations that can rob us of the joy of the ministry and render our churches ineffective. An unrealistic expectation arose in the early church when it seems to have been expected that the disciples would turn their attention from the ministry of the Word to the daily distribution for widows. One wonders how we would respond today in a situation like that of the Hellenists complaining about the distribution of food to the widows. Think of it another way: what would the apostles who refused to leave the attention of the Word to serve tables say if they saw some of the tasks we are performing?

There is a difference between realistic and unrealistic expectations. There is never an excuse for laziness or being slack in the ministry. It is realistic to expect that a pastor will work with excellence, be dependable, and devote themselves to the work of the ministry.

Sometimes unrealistic expectations become more important to congregations than Scriptural expectations. Unrealistic expectations arise from the view (usually a nonbiblical one) that people have about the duties of a pastor. They can come from a few people and be isolated, or may come from an entire congregation if based on tradition or the actions of previous pastors. They may be what you are expected to do (e.g., janitor, building contractor, landscaper, chauffeur) or even the level of expertise you are expected to have (e.g., high level of exposition for new pastor, professional counseling skills). They are often inconvenient, interrupting, and can result in hurt feelings, like the ire of a parishioner after you failed to visit their third cousin who lives two counties away. It is tempting to spend the time on the visit rather than deal with the ire. Consider the questions below and rate how true they are of you.[10]

I feel I can be myself in my work.

←--→

Rarely — Very Frequently

I am pleased with the importance my congregation attaches to the time I set aside for study.

←--→

Rarely — Very Frequently

I feel that I receive adequate recognition for the work I do.

←--→

Rarely — Very Frequently

The job requirements asked by the congregation utilize my training and capabilities very well.

←--→

Rarely — Very Frequently

Unrealistic expectations may involve how you do your work and how the congregation feels about your work. It can be disconcerting when the congregation does not value the work you have been trained to do and are biblically mandated to do. Unrealistic expectations do not just involve what you do, but may also involve how you do it.

These unrealistic expectations often carry over to the pastor's family. Again, sometimes these expectations arise from what a congregation has experienced from a previous pastor. At other times it is seen simply as an expectation of ministry, a "we hired two for the price of one" mentality like the pastor's wife quoted below.[11]

> "They have a standard that if you're a pastor's wife, you have to be there to participate in all of their activities."

This can leave a pastor and his family feeling unfairly criticized, frustrated, and unsupported by the congregation. This is often referred to as the fishbowl experience, which will be discussed later. Sometimes it seems like no matter what you do, someone will be dissatisfied.

> *For John the Baptist has come eating no bread and drinking no wine, and you say, "He has a demon." The Son of Man has come eating and drinking, and you say, "Look at him! A glutton and a drunkard, a friend of tax collectors and sinners!"*
>
> Luke 7:33-34

Jesus described this phenomenon when He pointed out how He and John the Baptist were criticized by the Pharisees. He pointed out the impossibility of pleasing some people. Too often in the ministry, we find ourselves in no win situations. No matter what we do, we displease some people. An example of this from my own ministry was a Super Bowl party we had one year in the church Fellowship Building. The leadership and I reasoned that the Super Bowl would be a wonderful time for people to get together, eat, fellowship, and watch a game. In the buildup to the party, some people approached the associate pastor and myself and expressed their concern that some of the commercials might not be appropriate for small children. As we planned for the event, we decided to play some Andy Griffith show reruns that we had instead of the commercials so the adults could chat and refill their nacho bowls while the kids were entertained.

As the Super Bowl got underway, we realized some missed the message that we would not be showing the commercials, and these same people only watched the Super Bowl for the commercials. Further, they were not fans of Andy Griffith. They were not happy.

As the game went on, these same people began asking whether we would watch the halftime show, which they wanted to see on the big screen. I began engaging in what cognitive behavioral theorists refer to as catastrophizing and wondered, "Is this the way Custer felt at the Battle of Little Bighorn?" Also, I had been reading a book on leadership about how a leader needed to be able to adapt in the middle of a situation, so I started wondering if we should stay the course. Quickly, I got the associate pastor and a deacon and we discussed our plight. We reasoned that the people who wanted to see the commercials were the same people who wanted to see the Super Bowl show, so we had already offended them. On the other hand, the parents and the little kids (who were our focus) were pleased with how everything was going, but if we changed course that would all change. Thankfully we decided to stay the course. By the way, this was Super Bowl XXXVIII with the infamous halftime show wardrobe malfunction. Staying the course was the right decision!

But in the spirit of a no win situation, word got back about someone who did not attend the Super Bowl party at the church. Apparently, they felt it was inappropriate to watch the Super Bowl in the Fellowship Building so they watched it at home instead. When the infamous wardrobe malfunction took place they gleefully wondered aloud how we handled it at the church. The ministry is filled with no win situations where no matter what you do you cannot satisfy everybody—or sometimes, anybody. All of this can result in a lot of stress. Consider the stress symptoms listed by Berry et al. on the next page.[12]

What symptoms of stress are you experiencing?

Tired all the time

←---→

Rarely | Very Frequently

Feeling down

←---→

Rarely | Very Frequently

Trouble sleeping

←---→

Rarely | Very Frequently

Headaches

←---→

Rarely | Very Frequently

Upset stomach

←---→

Rarely | Very Frequently

Lack of appetite

←---→

Rarely | Very Frequently

Bored

←---→

Rarely | Very Frequently

Unwanted weight loss

←---→

Rarely | Very Frequently

In toil and hardship, through many a sleepless night . . . And, apart from other things, there is the daily pressure on me of my anxiety for all the churches.

2 Corinthians 11:27-28

The Impact of Stress

When stress is not appropriately addressed, it can have a negative impact upon our physical, emotional, psychological, and even spiritual health. Stress probably impacts you more than you realize. For example, when we experience prolonged stress the result is increased activity in the genes involved in inflammation. This can impact your speech patterns. In one study, participants with more stress-related gene signatures talked less overall.[13]

Stress often makes us more susceptible to unhealthy eating and sedentary lifestyles. Stress seems to make us desire some type of reward like chocolate. However, the impact of stress makes these indulgences less enjoyable.[14]

One of the biggest physical symptoms of stress is sleep problems, which can impede our effectiveness in the ministry. For example, one study has indicated that losing just two hours of sleep per night can make you more irritable and easily frustrated.[15] We are more susceptible to overreacting to challenges when we have been sleep deprived. It makes me wonder whether Moses slept well the night before he struck the rock! There is no better example of the physical impact of stress than Jesus having blood in His sweat when He was at Gethsemane.

> *And being in agony he prayed more earnestly; and his sweat became like great drops of blood falling down to the ground.*
>
> Luke 22:44

This malady is called hematohidrosis and is a condition in which the capillary blood vessels that feed the sweat glands rupture, causing them to exude blood. This only occurs under conditions of extreme physical or emotional stress.[16] Jesus experienced the worst stress of all, and understands our difficulties (Hebrews 4:15).

Threats to Ministers: Burnout

Continuing to live beyond our limits leads to stress, which is followed by efforts to try harder, which only leads to burnout. It is too easy for pastors to get into this cycle. Pastors are especially vulnerable because much of what we do can result in emotional exhaustion, leaving us drained.[17]

Our approach to stress will increase or decrease our risk for burnout. A first step to dealing well with stress and preventing burnout (or recovering from it) is to know ourselves. There are certain situations that put us at risk for burnout.

Twenty-six percent of pastors report being at high or medium risk for burnout. However, the problem may be greater, since three-quarters of pastors say they know at least one pastor whose ministry ended as a result of stress.[18]

There are four personality dimensions that have been hypothesized to predict risk for burnout: desire to please others, guilt or shame orientation, being hard on oneself, and over identifying with your role.[19] Rate your susceptibility.

Risk for Desire to Please Others

Letting down others is a fear of mine

←---→

Rarely | Very Frequently

I have difficulty setting boundaries

←---→

Rarely | Very Frequently

For am I now seeking the approval of man, or of God? Or am I trying to please man? If I were still trying to please man, I would not be a servant of Christ.

Galatians 1:10

Desire to Please Others

It is healthy to frequently examine why you do what you do. Acting out of a desire to please others puts you at greater risk for burnout. There are many reasons why one might have a desire to please others. Most of us want to be liked and appreciated by our congregation. Where are you on the desire to please others continuum? If you are high on desire to please others you will be tempted to neglect spiritual disciplines, family, and hobbies in order to meet the demands of people in the church. You will also have trouble saying no to requests from others in the congregation that may be inappropriate and keep you away from fulfilling your ministry. For example, had the disciples been high in this area they might have chosen to become involved in the distribution of food to the widows rather than devoting themselves to preaching the Word of God (Acts 6:12). The Hellenists might have been happy with this, but the ministry would have suffered. Take the next survey on guilt and shame.

Risk for Guilt and Shame

I feel guilty when I take time for myself when there is something for parishioners that I should be doing

←---→

Rarely Very Frequently

I want all of my parishioners to like me

←---→

Rarely Very Frequently

But one thing I do: forgetting what lies behind and straining forward to what lies ahead, I press on toward the goal for the prize of the upward call of God in Christ Jesus.

Philippians 3:13b-14

Guilt and Shame

A second area of concern is guilt or shame proneness. It has been observed that pastors often struggle with a sense of shame that has been defined as a painful self-consciousness that one is less than what they want to be or think they should be. It is a sense of being "wrong." This "wrongness" leaves pastors feeling exposed, vulnerable, and unlovable.[20]

Where are you when it comes to being guilt and shame prone? A guilt-prone person tends to be concerned with how they can make amends. A shame-oriented person tends to be concerned with how they can hide their failures because they feel worthless and exposed. This orientation may result in one being especially fearful of making errors or not performing up to the expectations of others.[21] Paul likely felt guilt for how he had persecuted Christians in the past. Though he referred to this often, and it likely helped him as he endured persecution, he did not let his past inhibit his ministry efforts or produce a fear of failure.

Risk for Lack of Grace

I feel guilty when I err in some way in the ministry

←---→

Rarely Very Frequently

I tend to hide my mistakes because I am afraid of how I will be viewed

←---→

Rarely Very Frequently

Jesus said to him, "Feed my sheep."

John 21:17b

Lack of Grace for Yourself

Where are you when it comes to being hard on yourself? Lack of grace for yourself (being overly hard on yourself) places you at great risk for burnout. A willingness to give yourself some grace has been shown to be associated with less depression, self-criticism, rumination, thought suppression, and anxiety, and has been positively associated with well-being. Pastors who struggle in this area frequently say, "I should have." When people get mad at you, how do you handle it? When they criticize your family, how do you respond?

Research has indicated that clergy who are high on scales indicating they give themselves grace during times of stress or failure see themselves as connected with others. They are able to hold their worries in mindful awareness without ruminating, and are less likely to experience burnout.[22] After his spectacular failure of denying Jesus, Peter could have lived the rest of his life being too hard on himself. Rather than doing that, he got busy feeding the sheep (building the church) and connecting with others.

Risk for Role Differentiation

I see myself primarily as a pastor

←---→

Rarely Very Frequently

An overseer must be . . . the husband of one wife, He must manage his own household well. Moreover, he must be well thought of by outsiders.

1 Timothy 3:2b, 4a, 7a

Role Differentiation

How do you see yourself in your role as pastor? When a pastor is seen by everyone they encounter as a pastor, there is little role differentiation. This places one at greater risk for burnout. In one study, 55 percent of pastors who were more likely to be identified as a pastor in most of their encounters with people were more likely to neglect leisure, family, friends, and self-care.[23] How you think of yourself is especially important. Do you see yourself as a father and a husband as well as a pastor? The Scripture indicates that we are to nurture those roles as well; they actually help us become better pastors. Note the approach of the pastor quoted below.[24]

"I avoid becoming . . . emotionally dependent on the church."

Identify the area(s) where you are most susceptible to burnout. At a minimum, the impact of burnout can result in pastors being ineffective or can shorten their ministry because of the physical and psychological impact. However, burnout can have devastating spiritual consequences that can lead to falling into spectacular sin, ruining the ministry work of a pastor, harming their family, and damaging the church.

One can make a case for the events of 2 Samuel 11 being the result of a king suffering from burnout. David was no stranger to stress. From his time as a young shepherd he knew the stress of caring for sheep and protecting them from wild animals (1 Samuel 17:34-36). He battled lions and bears, which prepared him for his battle against the giant, Goliath (1 Samuel 17:37). David endured a lot of combat; after all, they would sing about him saying he had slain ten thousands (1 Samuel 18:7). David was forced to endure the tension that resulted from Saul's jealousy (1 Samuel 18:8) and eventually fled and hid in enemy territory (1 Samuel 19). Even after the death of Saul, and David's establishment as king, he was often under the inevitable stress of running a kingdom. Undoubtedly, David frequently felt like there was too much to do. He often neglected his family, and of course lived in a fishbowl.

In 2 Samuel 11, David appeared to be tired, bored, and ineffective when "it happened" with Bathsheba. David was either unwilling or too tired to deal with many important matters. When Amnon abused his sister Tamar (2 Samuel 13), David was angry but he did not hold Amnon accountable (2 Samuel 13:21), nor does it appear that he took the time to console Tamar (2 Samuel 13:20). When Absalom killed his brother, David never directly addressed the problem, leaving it to others to address (2 Samuel 14, 2 Samuel 18:15). Late in David's life, David's son Adonijah attempted to seize the throne (1 Kings 1). After David's death, Solomon had to deal with Adonijah (1 Kings 2:23-25). David failed to deal with Joab who worked against him in many ways (1 Kings 2:32), leaving this to Solomon. Based on 1 Kings 2, it does not appear that David ever effectively dealt with burnout. As a result, he suffered and his family and all of Israel were harmed.

We may have a lot in common with David. As we experience stress, we may become exhausted and overwhelmed. When we hear of a church member or leader who has behaved badly and even harmed others, we may be angered by what we hear but unwilling to confront or discipline the culprit or console those harmed. Rather than addressing issues and problems, we may be tempted to leave these for the next pastor or others to deal with. As a result, the pastor is diminished, their family may be neglected, and the church and the offending parties never become what God wants them to be. In the most difficult of these circumstances, a pastor might fall into ministry-ending sin.

Let us not make the same mistake. Let us deal with burnout. Let us be intentional about being balanced, effectively dealing with stress, and preventing or treating burnout. Decide now to intentionally protect yourself, your marriage, your family, and the church.

> *And, apart from other things, there is the daily pressure on me of my anxiety for all the churches.*
>
> 2 Corinthians 11:28

So let us go back to my question earlier. Are we hypocrites for preaching about the abundant life when we experience so much stress? When I read 2 Corinthians 11:28, I must admit I am a bit relieved to read that the Apostle Paul felt stress just like us as he experienced "daily pressure," and "anxiety for all the churches." According to Paul, the stress of the ministry is ever present. I am also relieved when I look at research on pastors. The majority of pastors in an old study from 1971 indicated that they experienced stress, often of a severe nature, for all of their years of ministry.[25] The key phrase was "all their years of ministry." In the ministry, stress never completely goes away. Perhaps the key question is, "can someone be under stress and also enjoy the abundant life?" Many (though, of course, not us) think the abundant life is filled with happiness, or perhaps even bliss.

Is This the Abundant Life?

Some were tortured, refusing to accept release, so that they might rise again to a better life. Others suffered mocking and flogging, and even chains and imprisonment. They were stoned, they were sawn in two, they were killed with the sword. They went about in skins of sheep and goats, destitute, afflicted, mistreated—of whom the world was not worthy—wandering about in deserts and mountains, and in dens and caves of the earth.

Hebrews 11:35b-38

The abundant life is not free of pain and suffering. If it were, Jesus, Paul, and those described in Hebrews 11 certainly missed out on the abundant life. I do not think that the presence of stress robs us of the abundant life Christ has for us. In fact, stress and trials seem to be not only intertwined with the abundant life, but even a requirement for the abundant life. Why else would James say, "Count it all joy . . . when you meet trials" if they do not help us? From James 1 you can conclude that life and the ministry actually should be stressful. It is through trials (and stress) that we develop.

> *Count it all joy, my brothers, when you meet trials of various kinds.*
>
> James 1:2

We do not feel like celebrating after the death of a key person in our church or an especially contentious period. But some of our most rewarding endeavors are filled with stress. It seems like nothing bonds us more with our congregation than going through trials together. It also seems like stress is inevitable with important work. Consider other occupations that are very stressful. First responders, medical professionals, law enforcement officers, and other occupations experience a lot of stress, largely because their decisions are often a matter of life and death for those with whom they interact. The noble minister can't help but feel stress on some level every day because they know the stakes are high. The ministry is more than an occupation. It is a mission that has eternal consequences as we represent the Lord Jesus Christ in our churches and to our community. We cannot help but experience stress as we struggle to minister well. The key is how we get intentional about dealing with the stress of ministry.

> "You got to take the long view with your ministry. You have to make priorities that are simply on top, like raising your own children and loving your own wife is more important than anything else you are doing. So you kind of set those priorities and don't make apologies for it."

Be Intentional

The pastor quoted above concluded that one must become very intentional about having a balanced approach to ministry and taking the long view.[26] Ask yourself where you want to end up in ministry. Balance will not just happen; it will require a disciplined approach of keeping the main things as the top priorities.

> *I am the vine; you are the branches. Whoever abides in me and I in him, he it is that bears much fruit, for apart from me you can do nothing.*
>
> John 15:5

Intentionally Take Time for God

There is a temptation to neglect the spiritual disciplines because we have so much to do. Indeed, a recent report of the Barna Group indicated that 47 percent of all pastors reported it was somewhat or very difficult to invest time in their own spiritual development.[27]

We cannot neglect the spiritual disciplines, or our work will be futile. We need not wonder what Jesus thinks about failing to spend time with Him. When Martha became upset because Mary was spending time with Jesus rather than serving, Jesus pointed out that she was anxious and troubled (Luke 10:41) about many things, but that Mary had chosen what was important. Spending time praying and reading the Word are key for us, but it is also good for the church.

Studies indicate that pastors who have a positive attitude toward prayer have a reduced risk for burnout.[28] Another study indicates that pastors who take time for Bible reading and prayer are less susceptible to stress. Having a time for retreat and solitude, as well as time for reading Scripture, journaling, fasting, and prayer, appears to help pastors be more effective. It has been hypothesized that pastors who engage in the spiritual disciplines function better because they are more likely to recognize their own limitations and realize that some situations are beyond their ability to solve.[29]

Jerry Bridges has suggested that pastors spend an hour a day with the Lord to feed their souls.[30] The first half is for reading and the second for prayer. His suggestion is supported in Scripture. Micah asked what God requires of us. The answer is that we walk humbly with the Lord (Micah 6:6-8). We see that Enoch did this and it pleased God (Genesis 5:21-24; Hebrews 11:5).

Further, meaningful worship at your church lowers your risk for burnout, relationship difficulties, and spiritual difficulties.[31] Time with the Lord solves and prevents a lot of problems. How can we have time to be intentional about the spiritual disciplines when we are so busy? As we discussed earlier, Jesus, too, was very busy; and though He was the Son of God (more spiritually mature than anyone), He did not neglect His time with the Father. Christ spent entire nights praying.

> *In these days he went out to the mountain to pray,*
> *and all night he continued in prayer to God.*
>
> Luke 6:12

Jesus' behavior shows us the importance of long periods of prayer before major decisions or events. Jesus prayed all night before selecting the disciples (Luke 6:13-16). We, too, would do well to spend significant periods praying before making major decisions (choosing who to mentor, dealing with a major conflict, or contemplating a move). Jesus seems to have a specific time and place where He prayed.

> *And rising very early in the morning, while it was still dark, he departed and went out to a desolate place, and there he prayed.*
>
> Mark 1:35
>
> *But he would withdraw to desolate places and pray.*
>
> Luke 5:16
>
> *And after he had taken leave of them, he went up on the mountain to pray.*
>
> Mark 6:46
>
> *Now about eight days after these sayings he took with him Peter and John and James and went up on the mountain to pray.*
>
> Luke 9:28

It appears that early in the morning was a favorite time of Jesus to pray. This is a good model for us, as it can help us get our day off to a good start. The Lord loved to pray in desolate places, places with no interruptions, places where it would be hard to find Him.

> **When and where do you pray?**
>
> **What do you need to be praying about?**

Some of these prayers involved great struggling. Prayer empowers us, but it can also be a struggle, especially when we complain to God about some of our difficulties. We learn from the epistles that Jesus struggled as He prayed.

> *In the days of his flesh, Jesus offered up prayers and supplications, with loud cries and tears, to him who was able to save him from death, and he was heard because of his reverence.*
>
> Hebrews 5:7

We can talk to the Lord about every problem that concerns us (Philippians 4:6) and ask Him to give us wisdom in how to deal with these issues (James 1).

> *Therefore an overseer must be . . . the husband of one wife . . . He must manage his own household well, with all dignity keeping his children submissive.*
>
> 1 Timothy 3:2, 4

Intentionally Take Time for Your Family

In the Barna Group survey, 43 percent of pastors are at high or medium risk for burnout when they are experiencing challenges in marriage, family, friendship, or other close relationships. The ministry can be difficult on a family. In one study, 26 percent of pastors reported experiencing marital problems and 27 percent reported parenting problems.[32]

We must meet the prerequisite requirements that a pastor be the husband of one wife and manage his household well (1 Timothy 3:2-5; Titus 1:6). This means we must make our marriages and our families a priority, lest we be in danger of being disqualified from ministry.

A strong and healthy family appears to be a key to successful ministry. Research on pastors indicate that their wives are their key supporters, and that effective pastors take time for their wife and family[33] as the pastor quoted next described.[34]

"I have a best friend wife . . .
We laugh together, we play together, we pray together."

Anecdotally, who has not had the experience of everyone telling them they have done well, only to have their wife be the one person who tells them the truth, helping them improve and effectively deal with many issues?

It takes time for us to love our wife. It is important personally to make time for our family, but also to model a loving relationship for the church. If we do not practice what we preach, our preaching will be ineffective.

Spending Time With Your Wife Is Not Optional

Husbands, love your wives, as Christ loved the church and gave himself up for her... In the same way husbands should love their wives as their own bodies. He who loves his wife loves himself... However, let each one of you love his wife as himself.

Ephesians 5:25, 28, 33a

Husbands, love your wives, and do not be harsh with them.

Colossians 3:19

If you look at Ephesians 5:28 through the lens of ministry, you might say, "If you love your ministry, you'll love your wife." The research indicates that pastors who report having healthy marriages tend to have established effective boundaries to make time with their wife and children a priority. Specifically, many are intentional about taking time to pray together, pray for one another, and read the Bible together.[35] Many effective pastors had special periods of time, even if they were short for one another as described below.[36]

"Every morning we as a family get to talk to each other.
'How are you?' 'Off you go,' those things."

Effective pastors provided stability and continuity, by staying put rather than moving frequently to other ministries. The research indicates that frequent moves to other churches are especially disruptive and stressful for families.[37]

Successful pastors refuse to accept unrealistic expectations of others in the congregation. These pastors often point to how they do not have a perfect family, and experience the same difficulties as others. Many congregations crave this kind of authenticity. There is an overall attitude of taking time for the family and an unwillingness to let anything get in the way of that time together. To keep the family healthy, family bonding time was considered valuable.[38]

Spending Time With Your Children Is Not Optional

...and his children are believers and not open to the charge of debauchery or insubordination.

Titus 1:6b

Fathers, do not provoke your children, lest they become discouraged.

Colossians 3:21

Fathers, do not provoke your children to anger, but bring them up in the discipline and instruction of the Lord.

Ephesians 6:4

Train up a child in the way he should go; even when he is old he will not depart from it.

Proverbs 22:6

You must model training your own children. Discipline them properly. Refuse to discipline them harshly even when you feel like they have embarrassed you.

A clergy family should share meaning not only with regard to its own identity, but the purpose of ministry. Does the family live according to a jointly held and articulated sense of mission? This is the best outcome for the family and the ministry.

Ministry can be tough on a family, but they are more likely to grow together. In the Barna Group report, half of pastors acknowledged that their current pastorate had been tough on their family.[39] However, pastors report greater marital and parental satisfaction than the general population. Only 19 percent indicated that pastoral ministry had a negative impact upon their family.[40] When you compare the marriage and parental satisfaction of pastors to the general population, you find that pastors are not doing so badly after all.[41]

Marital and Parental Satisfaction

	Pastors	General Population
With Marriage	70%	46%
With Parenting	60%	46%

Check out *First Aid for Your Emotional Hurts: Marriage*

Check out *First Aid for Your Emotional Hurts: Helping Children with Emotional Problems*

Jacob's well was there; so Jesus, wearied as he was from his journey, was sitting beside the well. It was about the sixth hour.

John 4:6

Intentionally Focus on Others

Again it is a relief to see that Jesus also understands the need to intentionally focus on others. His time with the Samaritan woman came at the sixth hour. Though He must have been exhausted, He took time to be with the Samaritan woman. This points to the importance of looking at a situation and taking time to evaluate whether it is from the Lord.

Therefore an overseer must be . . . hospitable.

1 Timothy 3:2

As a pastor, there are times we feel isolated. Often the problem is not that we do not have people around, but that we do not have the people we want around. We get tired of ministering to people. Jesus knew this.

We will talk more about mentoring later, but how is it that a pastor can get his work done when he seems to be interrupted so often by people? Again, we must meet the requirement of being hospitable. How do we follow that admonition while getting the work of the ministry completed?

J. Oswald Sanders tells about a busy man he knew who mastered the problem of interruptions. A visitor might say to him, "Well, I had two hours to kill here in between trains, and I thought I would come see you." The man would say, "The Lord must have brought you here. Let us find out why," and they would begin to pray. The interview took on greater importance and was often brief but pleasant.[42]

This is a good technique that can help our interactions be more profitable for the kingdom. As a pastor, we are tasked with equipping believers for ministry. We work with people, and we are always looking for able-bodied people who can serve. Jethro's solution to the overwork of Moses was that he search out able men.

> *Moses chose able men out of all Israel and made them heads over the people, chiefs of thousands, of hundreds, of fifties, and of tens. And they judged the people at all times. Any hard case they brought to Moses, but any small matter they decided themselves.*
>
> Exodus 18:25-26

The solution for the problem with the widows was the establishment of deacons.

> *Therefore, brothers, pick out from among you seven men of good repute, full of the Spirit and of wisdom, whom we will appoint to this duty.*
>
> Acts 6:3

We, too, want to look for able people to do ministries and then let them do it. In research on effective churches, one key was their ability to empower people to minister. One principle was that the people be able to do the ministry with 80 percent effectiveness. Too often, we do not have fellow ministers because we are dissatisfied with their performance. These verses remind me of a scene from *Band of Brothers.*

In Episode 7 of the *Band of Brothers, The Breaking Point* (at the 0:56:47 mark) the battle for Foy, Belgium is not going well. The lieutenant in charge of the attack is faltering and for a moment it looks like Captain Winters is going to enter the fray. At that point he is scolded by his commanding officer, "You are a battalion commander. Get back here!" Captain Winters then assigns another leader to the task.[43]

If you do not have people to help minister, pray for the Lord to send you people. That is what Jesus did when He had too much to do (Matthew 9:37-38). Then accept and celebrate whoever the Lord gives you to help with the ministry and step back. In research on comeback churches, the effective pastors were found to be very intentional about who they invested in.[44]

> *Now when Jesus heard this, he withdrew from there in a boat to a desolate place by himself. But when the crowds heard it, they followed him on foot from the towns.*
>
> Matthew 14:13

Intentionally Take Time for Yourself

God kept a Sabbath (Exodus 20:8-11), and we need one too. How does one take time for themselves when their primary work duties are on the Sabbath? Lately researchers have begun to put more emphasis on taking time off from work, since being unable to switch off work after hours is associated with burnout,[45] and having a period where one detaches from work results in higher life satisfaction.[46]

Just being able to get to a place where one does not have to think about work is restorative. Even Jesus took time to be by Himself even though He did not always succeed. His attempt shows we, too, need to make this effort and we will not always succeed.

After hearing the news of the death of John the Baptist, Jesus "withdrew from there in a boat to a desolate place by himself" (Matthew 14:13a). After a stressful situation we must look for opportunities to get away, even if it is briefly. This particular respite for Jesus was also brief, for the Scriptures say, "When the crowds heard it, they followed him" (Matthew 14:13b). So when you get a disturbing text while trying to take a walk in the park, or get a call about something while away on vacation, just remember Jesus understands.

Pastors with higher satisfaction with activities outside of the ministry, such as leisure and exercise, are also less susceptible to burnout.[47] Further, the research indicates that we are more effective after a break. Since we are often engaged in high intensity living, sometimes our hopes are placed in a vacation or some other trip where we can be refreshed. This is why we are especially stressed when we cannot relax on these excursions because a ministry need arises.[48]

We should all take vacations. However, vacations only have small positive effects, with the benefits declining within a few weeks of returning to work.[49] A vacation is like sleeping in on a Saturday. That extra sleep does not mitigate the damage of sleep deprivation the rest of the week, so a few days of rest do not mitigate the damage of failing to take time off during the year.[50]

It would benefit us personally and enhance our ministry if we were intentional about taking time for regular breaks. When you find yourself struggling to get anything done, take a break. This is often far more effective than just pushing through that time period and trying to crank work out.[51]

Focusing our attention too long on something is more likely to wear us out. This is often referred to as neural fatigue, which is the buildup of waste matter in the brain. This makes it more difficult for us to function well. You might think of it as your mental fuel tank being empty.[52]

Taking regular breaks can help you deal better with stressors. Even short breaks can help you perform better. In the research, this is referred to as "microbreaks" of a few minutes that can improve mood or attention. A microbreak may consist of talking briefly to a friend, having a snack, reading the news for a few minutes, listening to music, watching a brief video, or even sitting quietly.[53]

You may need to seek the assistance of others to help you determine what kinds of breaks you need to take. People often are poor judges of the type of breaks that help them the most. In some cases, there has been a disconnect between the kind of break people enjoyed the most and the break that provided the most relief from stress. For example, one study indicated that some people preferred a walk in the park, but monitoring of individuals indicated that doing some relaxation exercise actually worked better for them.[54]

On the other hand, taking a break and doing something you enjoy does appear to help improve well-being with fewer health symptoms like eye strain and headaches. Lastly, and somewhat surprisingly, breaks seem to be more effective in the morning by restoring energy and reducing health symptoms.[55]

What kinds of breaks are good for you? Choose something that is not too similar to the work you are doing. Breaks that involve exercise and spending time in natural settings are good bets.[56]

> *And behold, there arose a great storm on the sea, so that the boat was being swamped by the waves; but he was asleep.*
>
> Matthew 8:24

Intentionally Focus on Your Sleep

Sometimes the difficulties of the ministry make it hard for us to sleep well. Someone calls late at night to complain about something or discuss a problem they are having, and it may be difficult to sleep (or go back to sleep) afterward. Perhaps you find yourself tossing and turning in the night as you worry about finances or dwell on criticism. The ministry can be tough on your sleep, and yet you desperately need to sleep better. Losing just two hours of sleep can result in increased irritability and speaking before you think. This compounds your problems. You desperately need your sleep. Sleep is one of the most helpful actions for dealing with stress. A good night of sleep can serve as a way to clean your brain of toxins.[57]

But how can you sleep when you are under stress? Jesus is the model. He kept trying to get away from the crowds (Mark 4:35-36), and on one occasion when He was on a boat, a windstorm arose. He was so tired He slept as the boat incurred damage (Mark 4:36b-38) until the disciples awakened Him.

The account of Jesus sleeping in the midst of a storm is recorded in Mark 4, Matthew 8, and Luke 8. In Luke 8, the incident is recorded right after a bit of friction between Jesus and "his mother and brothers" (Luke 8:19-21). This is just the kind of thing that causes many of us to have trouble sleeping (Luke 8:22-25). Yet Jesus was able to sleep, even in the middle of a storm. We, too, can sleep even in the midst of a stormy ministry season.

Perhaps the only way to rest in these kinds of situations is to have the unwavering hope that God will make a way for your needs and the needs of others to be met. So we may need to focus closely on the passages we frequently share with others in their time of need. You may know that whatever you read, watch, or think about during the one to two hours before you go to bed tends to stick with you through the night. So if you receive a distressing phone call, you want to counteract that. We tend to think about these things even though we are unaware of doing so. Interestingly, David referred to this long before we had sleep studies.

> *My soul will be satisfied as with fat and rich food,*
> *and my mouth will praise you with joyful lips,*
> *when I remember you upon my bed,*
> *and meditate on you in the watches of the night;*
> *for you have been my help,*
> *and in the shadow of your wings I will sing for joy.*
>
> Psalm 63:5-7

It would be good for us to focus on Scripture before we try to go to sleep. Here are a few examples of passages to think about.

> *Do not be anxious about anything, but in everything by prayer and supplication with thanksgiving let your requests be made known to God. And the peace of God, which surpasses all understanding, will guard your hearts and your minds in Christ Jesus.*
>
> Philippians 4:6-7

Immediately before bedtime, pray about anything that bothers you. If you continue to have trouble, write out your prayers. Another helpful passage is Proverbs 16:3.

> *Commit your work to the Lord,*
> *and your plans will be established.*
> Proverbs 16:3

Talk to the Lord about your plans and difficulties and trust Him. I also like Psalm 16:8.

> *I have set the Lord always before me;*
> *because he is at my right hand, I shall not be shaken.*
> Psalm 16:8

Use the Word of God to combat your fears, and watch your sleep problems dissipate. Earlier, we saw there were times when Jesus prayed all night, and we may too, on occasion. Yet there is a major difference between worrying all night and praying all night. We need to pray more and worry less. For more about the value of sleep and good sleep hygiene see *First Aid for Your Health—Making 10 Therapeutic Life Changes.*

Intentionally Focus on Your Health

You have one body, and that body helps or hinders you as you engage in ministry. Many pastors have not been good stewards of their health. Pastors appear to be at a greater risk for obesity and its fallout of chronic health conditions. A study of United Methodist clergy indicated 10 percent higher obesity rates than the general population. This equated to higher rates of lifestyle-related health problems like diabetes, hypertension, asthma, and arthritis.[58] Similar rates have been reported among the Evangelical Lutheran Church in America.[59] In another study, a third (34%) of U.S. Protestant pastors were found to be obese. Further, bivocational pastors were nearly twice as likely as other pastors to be obese. Researchers believe the reason for the problem is a lack of a Sabbath or time off because a pastor lowers their risk for obesity by 92 percent just by taking a Sabbath.[60]

So taking a short break to rest is not just important for our minds, allowing us to break free, but it also helps our health. If you do not take time for yourself you will be less effective and may even see your ministry shortened.

It is a good idea to be intentional about how to incorporate an activity into your break so that you will receive a health benefit as well. Being physically active is especially beneficial to your health. The Center for Disease Control recommends 150 minutes a week of moderate physical activity.[61]

Some may ask, "Was Jesus physically active?" I do not believe He had a treadmill or jogged, but in reading the gospels He does appear to walk a lot. Some have suggested that He walked 20 miles a day, which equates to over 42,000 steps a day. Considering that we try to get most people to take 10,000 steps a day (and struggle to get that), it looks like He did not need a treadmill.

Too many pastors claim they do not have time for a daily activity. Perhaps you can incorporate more activity into the regular activities of your day. For example, you might take the stairs rather than the elevator and walk every opportunity you get. Will taking the time to be more active diminish your ministry output? Consider that the Apostle Paul wrote 13 of the 27 books of the Bible, and yet he likely traveled some 10,000 miles on foot.[62] Being active helps you be more productive. What is an activity you can engage in for at least 20 minutes a day?

What works for you?

___ Run outside	___ Run on the treadmill
___ Bike	___ Golf
___ Hunt	___ Fish
___ Tennis	___ Garden
___ Play a sport	___ Shoot pool
___ Swim	___ Bowl

I want to encourage you to consider walking. Walking seems to help whatever ails a person. Walkers even sleep better.[63] Dennis Wiggs, a long-time pastor in North Carolina, once described his walking regimen to me. It was a great physical benefit to him but he also noted, "I worked out many problems walking up and down the road." Walkers tend to be better at problem-solving. Somewhere during a walk, a problem is put into perspective. Walkers are also goal and action oriented and more creative. Ideas sometimes just come to us as we walk. It is said that Thomas Jefferson habitually walked to clear his thoughts. Through history many have described this phenomenon.[64]

Latin proverb: *Solvitur ambulando = It is solved by walking*

"When I stop I cease to think; my mind only works with my legs."
Jean-Jacques Rousseau,1782, Confessions

Whatever activity you use note that there is value to getting outside to get some fresh air. For example, people tend to view indoor activities as more strenuous than outdoor activities. Further, they tend to rate their mood higher after engaging in an outdoor activity than an indoor activity.[65]

Both cardiovascular exercise and resistance training seem to be effective in preventing burnout.[66] But choose an activity that works for you. The kind of activity you engage in can serve as a short break from your stress. This decreases your likelihood of burnout, depression, and health problems. Remember, the activity need not be strenuous only enjoyable but just 20 minutes a day of moderate exercise (e.g., walking, gardening) produces the benefit.[67] The key is to get moving.

Check out *First Aid for Your Health: Making 10 Therapeutic Life Changes.*

Making the best use of the time, because the days are evil.
Ephesians 5:16

Intentionally Use Your Time

Many people respond to stress by working harder, which increases their susceptibility to burnout. Sometimes it is hard to know how to respond to the demands on our time. We are called to be servants, and we see this modeled in the Scripture. Moses is always referred to as the Lord's servant (Numbers 12:7, Joshua 1:2). Jesus reminded us that He came to be a servant (Mark 10:45), and Paul commanded us to serve one another (Galatians 5:13). As we deal with the problems that come our way we can quickly become overwhelmed when we have too much to do and unrealistic expectations. Yes, we are to serve, but we must serve by doing the right things. We must serve wisely. In the section on *First Aid for Failure*, we will look at tasks that we are called upon to perform.

How isolated are you?

←---→

Very (I have no one to confide in) Not at all (plenty of support)

I can trust my deacon/elder board (superiors) to keep confidences.

←---→

Rarely true Almost always true

Threat to Ministers and Their Families: Loneliness

How would you rate yourself on the items above?[68] Who can you talk to about the difficulties you experience in the ministry? Sometimes it seems like no one understands what you are experiencing. Sometimes it is hard to know who you can trust and who will keep something confidential. The ministry can be a lonely place. If you are lonely, you are in good company. A. W. Tozer said, "Most of the world's greatest souls have been lonely." It has been reported that years ago when pastors wrote into *Focus on the Family,* 70 percent indicated they did not have a close friend or confidant.[69] In one study, 55 percent of pastors indicated that pastoral ministry made them feel lonely at times. Younger pastors were more likely to be lonely than older pastors. Pastors of larger churches (250 and above) were also more likely to report feeling lonely.[70] One reason for this loneliness is that pastors and their families can be isolated. Sometimes it may feel like everything you do is scrutinized. Consider the statement below.[71]

> "It's like we're inside an aquarium, where everything is looked at, our movements . . . like a fish . . . the church members observe its movements, its looks, something like that."

The Fishbowl Experience

The above description by the wife of a pastor points to what is often referred to as the fishbowl experience, where a family feels like their every move is being watched and scrutinized. The fishbowl experience is not confined to the ministry. Politicians, media personalities, and musical artists all know the fishbowl experience. How often does a pastor have something in common with a politician or a rock star? Unfortunately, the attention can lead to interpersonal struggles for the family, especially when they feel judged and undermined by people in the church.[72]

The fishbowl experience can put extreme pressure on the marriage as the family begins to think about how their actions may be perceived by others. Usually their peers or family are unfamiliar with this kind of scrutiny unless they grew up in a ministry family. It is hard to be thrust into a situation where your every move and word is being evaluated for the impact they can have in a church setting.[73] The scrutiny even reaches the children.[74]

> "It's like the children are being dictated upon . . . I feel that the children are suffering too, it's like they can't move freely."

Sometimes resentment can develop when a family member begins to compare their experience to those of their peers. After all, a teen may think, "I wasn't called into the ministry." Read the description below.[75]

> "Like in church, you have to behave well. You should know those things since you're a pastor's kid. You are not supposed to make a mistake, something like that. That's what burdened me most in my childhood, being a child of a pastor. People expect a lot from you. Like if you did something wrong, it's a big deal, unlike if you're a normal youth."

The scrutiny can also feel unfair. This is likely what the pastor I spoke to from another country (mentioned in the first pages of this book) was referring to when he said that some children of pastors had no interest in entering the ministry. What has the impact been upon you and your family? Answer two of the items from Faucett et al.'s survey.[76]

I feel that my family really would like for me to be in another job

←---→

Rarely true — Almost always true

I feel my wife or children have been criticized unfairly by a congregant

←---→

Rarely — Very Frequently

This phenomenon is one of the hardest to deal with in the ministry. Moses also knew this stress. Moses was criticized over his wife (Numbers 12:1-2), though this was really an attack on him. Some will attack your family to get at you.

Jesus had to deal with the fishbowl experience. An example is found in Matthew 15:1-2 where the Pharisees and scribes were critical of Him since His disciples did not wash their hands.

> *Then Pharisees and scribes came to Jesus from Jerusalem and said, "Why do your disciples break the tradition of the elders? For they do not wash their hands when they eat."*
>
> Matthew 15:1-2

Rather than focusing upon the people Jesus had healed in the previous chapter (Matthew 14:34-36), these people focused on how Jesus' disciples ate their food. The disciples were the family of Jesus (Mark 3:31-35). When the disciples were attacked, it was an attack on Jesus' family. If you were Jesus, how would you feel? I would be thinking, "Can't you focus on something more important?" The disciples were criticized for violating a tradition rather than the Scripture. Even today, it is often the violation of a particular tradition that leads to criticism. We have just helped someone after an unexpected death in their family or are discipling a new believer when someone criticizes something one of our family members has said or done.

The fishbowl experience combined with the critical attitude of some congregants may lead pastors and their families to believe they have no one with whom they can talk. Some families may withdraw from their congregation. Indeed, many pastors warn those new to the ministry not to befriend others in their congregation. No doubt this has arisen out of ministry families being attacked by those who have gotten close to them and turned against them. This is a dangerous approach. Consider the statement below.[77]

> "I want to have someone whom I can always talk to even about personal things. It's just that it can't really be with a member."

We can begin to feel as if we cannot share our problems with anyone in the church. The quote below indicates one reason is that people do not really understand that ministry families have the same kinds of problems.

> "I never ask for help from the members since not all of them can understand the situation... others say that since I'm a pastor's wife I shouldn't be experiencing those negative things."

We need to resist the urge to isolate ourselves. We need others, even people within our churches, since the effects of stress are moderated by the presence of congregational support.[79]

We need support from the congregation to function well in ministry. No doubt we need to feel we are not alone.[80] Having friends one can talk to who listen and provide suggestions lessens the negative effects of the stressors of ministry.[81]

> *Whoever isolates himself seeks his own desire;*
> *he breaks out against all sound judgment.*
> Proverbs 18:1

Know Your Risk

So what can you do to avoid being isolated? Know your specific risks. The ministry naturally places you at risk for loneliness, but other factors like where you live and how long you attended school have a lot to do with your risk for loneliness. If you live in an area where there are fewer believers, your risk for loneliness increases. For example, pastors in the Northeast are 20 percent more likely to have no close friends; those living in the South have a 10 percent likelihood of no close friends; and those in the West are 9 percent likely to have no close friends. Further, pastors with a graduate degree are more likely than pastors with at most a Bachelor's degree to have three to five close friends (41 to 33 percent).[82]

Your personality also plays a role in your risk level. Rediger has written extensively about loneliness in the ministry and hypothesized that there are four different ways in which pastors socialize with their congregants.[83] There are gregarious pastors who live to be with people and will struggle when they are not. On the surface, it appears they are at less risk for loneliness, but they are especially susceptible when there is turmoil within the congregation or someone who does not like them.

There are selective pastors who choose when to be with people and when to be alone. The interaction is often based on particular circumstances. There are private pastors who prefer to be alone, but are with others when that is appropriate. Then there are detached pastors who insist on being alone and to function with a minimum interaction with others. This person would prefer to do their work on their own.

Identify your risk level and develop a plan, because no matter what your type, you need some friends. Loneliness is bad for your ministry and your health. In general, it is clear that having more friends makes us healthier, while loneliness has been tied to many health problems. Research on superagers (adults over 80 who have cognitive abilities of a much younger person) indicates that they have strong social networks or positive relations with others.[84] Remaining isolated over time results in a decrease in heart rate variability, which places you at greater risk for developing cardiac problems later in life.[85] Identify people you can talk to below.

Who can you talk to?

___ Friends	___ Your wife
___ Other pastors	___ Deacons/Elders
___ Extended family	___ Counselor
___ Denominational official	___ Other

. . . he must not be arrogant or quick tempered . . but hospitable . .

Titus 1:7b, 8:a

Soberly Assess Your Situation

If you feel isolated, is there really no one that you can talk to? Are your really isolated? Elders are required to be sober-minded. We do not talk a lot about being sober-minded. When Paul wrote to Timothy to be sober, he was not just talking to him about his temper and avoiding substances. We must use sober judgement about loneliness as well. Sometimes we are not accurately assessing our situation. That was the case with Elijah. Elijah appears to have felt lonely and isolated, which contributed to his ministry breakdown.

Then Elijah said to the people, "I, even I only, am left a prophet of the Lord, but Baal's prophets are 450 men.

1 Kings 18:22

I, even I only, am left, and they seek my life, to take it away.
I, even I only, am left, and they seek my life, to take it away.

1 Kings 19:10b, 14b

Elijah claimed to be alone frequently. Sometimes we act like we are alone but we really are not alone. In 1 Kings 18, we see there were others who followed the Lord when Elijah met Obadiah. Obadiah was clearly on Elijah's side. He had courageously saved the lives of 100 prophets (1 Kings 18:4).

> *And as Obadiah was on the way, behold, Elijah met him. And Obadiah recognized him and fell on his face and said, "Is it you, my lord Elijah?"*
>
> 1 Kings 18:7

Elijah did not appear to make an effort to befriend Obadiah, and Obadiah does not seem to think Elijah valued his life (1 Kings 18:9). This was a missed opportunity for Elijah to have companionship with another believer. Elijah felt he was alone when he really was not alone, but that was his choice. When Elijah deteriorated he again described how he was alone. When he encountered trouble he left his servant (1 Kings 19:3) and isolated himself in a cave (1 Kings 19:9). When he continued to complain that no one else followed the Lord, God confronted him and pointed out that there were 7,000 who had not bowed to Baal (1 Kings 19:18). He did not need to be lonely.

Are we really as lonely as we think? In the Barna Group report, pastors were asked if they felt well-supported by those close to them. Sixty-eight percent said frequently, 29 percent said sometimes, and only 4 percent said seldom or never. On the other hand, when the same question was asked of U.S. adults, 43 percent said frequently, 35 percent said sometimes, and 23 percent said seldom or never. Maybe we are in better shape than we think. Pastor satisfaction with friends is on par or slightly better than the U.S. average.[86]

It appears that pastors actually have a greater amount of supportive relationships inside their congregations than outside. This seems to contradict conventional wisdom. Cautions about pastors befriending church members come from anecdotes which may not generalize to the day-to-day experiences of the majority of clergy.[87]

It is true that we cannot share every detail of our struggles with people within the church, but that does not mean we must detach ourselves from them either. They do not have to know every detail or we need not tell them the nature of every issue for them to provide support.

There is no doubt, however, that at times we will feel lonely. The Lord truly knew loneliness, and He could say no one understood what He went through. At His most difficult hour (Matthew 26:40), He did not have anyone who would take the time to pray for or with Him. Later, He was abandoned by Peter, His top supporter, when Peter denied Him three times (Luke 22:54-62). Jesus truly knows how we feel.

> *Iron sharpens iron, and one man sharpens another.*
>
> Proverbs 27:17

Find a Mentor

So what can you do if you feel isolated in the ministry? I encourage you to actively seek someone who will mentor you. The research indicates that those who actively seek mentors have a lower risk for burnout.[88] You probably already know how important mentoring is. In one study, 45 percent of pastors mentioned the need to be mentored more by others.[89] A mentor can challenge you. A mentor can say, "the last four times I have seen you, you have said you are tired. Have you noticed that pattern?"[90]

What do you look for in a mentor? The first step (and probably the hardest) is someone who is willing to mentor you and who is growing themselves. Unfortunately, that can narrow the pool of potential mentors down. However, it only takes one person. Ideally you will look for and find a person who has been where you are and is now where you would like to be. In other words, you are looking for someone who has served in the kind of church you are serving in at the moment and has been successful at the transitioning of that church. People who are in a similar situation as you can listen to you, which can relieve stress, but they may be unable to challenge you and help you grow. It can actually be dangerous if you are mentored by someone who is not as far along as you. Consider the example of King Rehoboam, who sought the advice of his friends after he became king. He listened to them rather than the wise counsel he received from older men (1 Kings 12:6-8). As a result, the kingdom was split (1 Kings 12:16-20).

Many churches have split after pastors have taken the same type of advice. It would be like a new pastor talking to some of his wise elders about a move he was considering making and ignoring their advice and taking greater risks or quicker moves than he would without that advice. Interestingly, in the research from breakout churches, the churches that grew made changes after thoroughly thinking them through.[91] You have to change, but you need to thoroughly consider the implementation of that change.

I have had the opportunity of working with professors and other leaders to examine the mentoring process. I have observed that assistant professors do not mentor other assistant professors well (they are too similar). I have also learned that sometimes professors do not mentor assistant professors as well (the gap between them is too big). But associate professors mentor assistant professors well because they are not too far removed from the problems the professors one rank below have, and they have experienced success dealing with these issues. There may be times when an assistant professor or a full professor can help, but as a whole, the assistant professor needs an associate professor and the associate professor needs a full professor.

In a church setting, this would be like having someone who has been in a church that is about the size of yours, and who has experienced growth over a period. They would be more helpful to you than someone at a church the same size and with similar years of experience or a pastor from a much larger church who would be dealing with an entirely different set of problems than the ones you face. So choose your mentor well; a well selected mentor who is wise and willing will be invaluable to your ministry.

> *So he departed from there and found Elisha.*
>
> 1 Kings 19:19a

Be a Mentor

What if you are unable to find a mentor? It is possible that you will not be able to find someone to mentor you, especially if you are further along in the ministry. It seems this was the case with Elijah who was well along in his ministry when he had trouble. Could you mentor someone else? Sometimes when I talk to people about mentoring they point out that no one ever mentored them. We have been called to serve (Mark 10:43-45). If we assist and mentor someone else, we just might find that mentoring or helping them also helps us. After Elijah became so disappointed and discouraged that he quit the ministry, God instructed him to mentor Elisha. The relationship played a major role in changing the lives of both Elijah and Elisha. The Lord's solution for Elijah's loneliness was to find someone to mentor.

> "I feel unfulfilled because of a lack of visible results."
> **Disappointed Pastor**

Threat to Pastors: Disappointment and Discouragement

The pastor quoted above said what many are thinking. Discouragement is common for ministers.[92] In one study, 55 percent of pastors reported that it was easy for them to become discouraged in the ministry.[93] Another study found that 43 percent of pastors said disappointment was the greatest challenge they faced in the ministry.[94] Let us take a look at this discouragement and determine what we can do about it.

> *O Lord, you have deceived me, and I was deceived.*
> Jeremiah 20:7a

Lack of Church Growth

Several years ago, I surveyed pastors about how fulfilled they felt in the ministry. A common theme was a feeling of unfulfillment because they were not seeing the results they expected for their efforts. I have experienced this. I carry a bookbag everywhere I go. If I could go back in time, I suspect there would have been a copy of several books and articles on church growth that I was carrying around. I was on a mission and expected everyone to respond to the gospel and our church to explode. I remember a big outreach event we had where many people came out. Afterward, we were filled with excitement, and my father-in-law remarked, "You will have a church full on Sunday!" He said what all of us were thinking. It did not go that way though. Results seemed difficult to achieve and slower than anticipated. Sometimes it was hard to discern progress.

There is no escaping the impact slow church growth (or even decline) has upon a pastor. A recent study indicated that a large number of pastors depend on their church's growth for their own personal affirmation.[95] So, if you are pastoring one of the eight out of ten churches in the U.S. that are declining or have plateaued, that does not bode well.[96]

Pastors are more likely to feel inadequate about their work than other occupations, as can be seen in the box below.[97]

Feeling Inadequate About Work

	Frequently	Sometimes	Seldom/Never
Pastors	12%	45%	42%
General Population	08%	22%	70%

Unsurprisingly, 55 percent of pastors who are in churches where attendance is declining report being disappointed in their current ministry, compared to only 18 percent of pastors in growing churches.[98] When asked about their church, many pastors put on a strong face and describe a rosy picture while they are actually crushed in their spirit.

There is a perception that most churches are exploding in attendance and operating multiple sites. But this is not what most pastors and churches are experiencing. In fact, there is a downward trend overall in worship attendance in the United States. Though the population of the United States is growing, worship attendance is not keeping pace. From 1990 to 2010, there was a 24 percent population gain in the United States; however, there was only an average annual growth rate of 1.1 percent for worship attendance.[99]

This results in an environment where many will be disappointed by their ministry and struggle with discouragement. Where do you rate yourself on some of the questions from Berry et al. and Lee and Iverson-Gilbert clergy work?[100]

This Is Me

I worry about the lack of growth in our church

←---→

Rarely true — Almost always true

I feel ineffective

←---→

Rarely true — Almost always true

There is a gap between my expectations and reality

←---→

Rarely true — Almost always true

What kind of discouragement do you face? When our church does not grow as rapidly as we think it should, it often results in us feeling ineffective—especially when there is a gap between our expectations and reality. A sense of this is seen in Elijah when Israel does not seem to be following God after the victory at Mount Carmel. A key statement is, "I am no better than my fathers" (1 Kings 19:4b). Perhaps Elijah looked at himself and thought he would succeed in the ministry where his fathers or predecessors had failed. He was disappointed and discouraged.

You may wonder: has there ever been a time as challenging as the one we minister in today? The prophet Jeremiah might think so. Jeremiah once told the Lord that he had been deceived by God about what he could expect in the ministry. Jeremiah served in a difficult ministry for 40 years (Jeremiah 1:1-3). He was probably called into the ministry around age 20. He prophesied for 18 years and 3 months during the time of Josiah, but his ministry became much more difficult after King Josiah was killed in battle.

If ever there was a minister who worked hard but did not see results, it was Jeremiah. You can almost feel him weeping as you read the pages of the book of Jeremiah. At least none of us will likely experience the level of discouragement he did—his nation collapsed on his watch and there are no obvious converts reported throughout his book.

> *So you shall speak all these words to them, but they will not listen to you. You shall call to them, but they will not answer you.*
>
> Jeremiah 7:27

Lack of Influence

Many pastors are also disappointed by a lack of influence in their community and their own church. Young people seem to be leaving the church. Numbers of those who believe in cults, other religions, and even nothing in particular are on the rise.[101] Christianity (and the input of pastors) is not valued as it once was. A recent opinion poll indicated that Americans have a lower view of clergy than at any other time. Even self-identified Christians do not seem to have a high opinion of pastors, with 43 percent rating the ethical standards of clergy as just average.[102]

Our situation seems bad, but Jeremiah might say we say we have not seen anything. In his ministry he had the bad experience of people refusing to listen to him as well, and he could not influence his community to follow the Lord.

> *And Elijah came near to all the people and said, "How long will you go limping between two different opinions? If the Lord is God, follow him; but if Baal, then follow him." And the people did not answer him a word.*
>
> 1 Kings 18:21

Disappointed in People

Both Jeremiah and Elijah knew the disappointment of working with people. Pastoral work is people work, so there are many opportunities for disappointment. The growth of the church hinges on the decisions of our people, and whether they are faithful and committed. Too often we see them wander from the faith or church, chasing travel ball with their kids or weekends at the mountains or beach. In the Barna Group report, the worst part of the pastor's job was identified as lack of commitment among laypeople (35%), and low spiritual maturity among church goers (27%).[103] Pastors invest their time doing weddings, funerals, and hospital visitation for people and families, which often do not materialize into church members or even attenders. Pastors seem to be especially disappointed when they have poured their lives into people who head off to bigger and assumingly better churches after their lives have stabilized. I suspect every pastor knows this feeling (even the one who pastors the church they go off to). Pastors tend to struggle in silence lest they come across as whining.

The Prophet Elijah was certainly disappointed in his people. Clearly he hoped Israel would turn to the Lord. Could he have thought Ahab and even Jezebel would repent? Note that when he saw things as they were (1 Kings 19:3), that is when he became very discouraged.

In our ministry, this would be like planning and hoping for many in our church or community to get right with the Lord, then a dramatic event takes place and it appears that these individuals have repented only to learn later they had not repented at all. Another example might be having a meeting over a conflict years in the making (that previous pastors had failed to resolve), and believing the issue had been resolved, only to see later that nothing had been resolved at all. That may be what Elijah referred to when he said, "I am no better than my fathers" (1 Kings 19:4b).

> *God relented of the disaster that he had said he would do to them, and he did not do it. But it displeased Jonah exceedingly, and he was angry.*
>
> Jonah 3:10b–4:1

Disappointed in Their Ministry

If there ever were a minister dissatisfied with his assignment, it was Jonah. In fact, he rejected his ministry assignment (Jonah 1:1-3). You might say Jonah was unwilling to answer his call until God intervened (Jonah 2). But even then he was not happy about it, and after he succeeded he voiced his displeasure to God (Jonah 4:1-3).

Jonah was a very successful prophet. He preached and a whole city repented. However, it is unlikely that Jonah's actions would have been celebrated by his peers since Nineveh was an enemy of Israel. It is also unlikely that Jonah had dreamed of ministry in Nineveh. He seems to have been a "flag waving" prophet who prophesied about Israel's expansion (2 Kings 14:25). He would have preferred to minister in Israel.

What do you have in common with Jonah? Perhaps you are dissatisfied with where you find yourself ministering. There is nothing flashy about your ministry or anything that gets the attention of others. Maybe there is no one who would really like to trade places with you. Suppose you find yourself ministering to a congregation primarily over 50 and you long for a more youthful congregation. It is very important work, but it is not what you dreamed of doing. It is a bit like Jonah's call.

The data suggests that pastors can be discouraged by how their church is perceived. For example, the pastor of an established church can be discouraged when a new church with dynamic youth ministries opens nearby, and a congregation suddenly finds itself feeling "gray."[104]

No doubt the size of a church can be a disappointment to a pastor as well. Thirty-four percent of those who pastor churches with less than 100 people in attendance report disappointment, and 37 percent of those who pastor churches with between 100 and 250 people report being disappointed, compared to 15 percent of large church pastors who report disappointment.[105]

Are you the one who is to come,
or shall we look for another?"

Matthew 11:3b

Disappointment Can Lead to Doubt

Pastors can be disappointed when they feel ineffective in the ministry. We can be disappointed by other people, and that disappointment and discouragement can lead to doubt. This can even degenerate to a point where one struggles with their faith. In the Barna Group research, 24 percent of pastors said they had experienced a period during their ministry when they significantly doubted their faith.[106]

Do you fit that category? Do you know anyone that fits that category? How about John the Baptist? John the Baptist is a profile in discouragement (Matthew 11). John's birth was a miracle; he leapt at the announcement of Jesus' birth. He had been prophesied about in Malachi 3:1, and he was like Elijah (Malachi 4:5). At the beginning of his ministry he effectively preached to a diverse group of people (Mark 1:1-8). As he was preaching, Jesus approached him and had John baptize Him, and John recognized Jesus as the Messiah (John 1:29-34).

As John the Baptist saw the lives of people being changed, do you think he thought, "And we are just getting started"? It is unlikely he realized that was the best, most exciting phase he would ever see in the ministry. Whatever he thought, it is clear that he was disappointed when he sent the message to Jesus asking, "Are you the one who is to come, or shall we look for another?" (Matthew 11:3). Who could blame him? He was in the dungeon of a prison (his personality type was to be outdoors), and he was hearing about all of the miracles Jesus was performing (Matthew 11:2)—he could use a little of that, he probably thought. Even worse, he was suffering (and about to be executed) while wicked men like Herod were free to do as they liked. He did not like it, so he sent that question by messengers. In essence he asked, "Are you the Messiah, or should we be looking for someone else? Tell me, has my ministry been in vain?" Disappointment had knocked that "Behold the Lamb of God" message right out of him. He was about as low as one can go. Disappointment had led to doubt.

But he himself went a day's journey into the wilderness and came and sat down under a broom tree. And he asked that he might die, saying, "It is enough; now, O Lord, take away my life, for I am no better than my fathers."

1 Kings 19:4

Disappointment Can Lead to Depression

Disappointment left unaddressed can even lead to depression. According to the Barna Group report, almost half of pastors have faced depression. In one study, pastors were twice as likely to struggle with depression as the general population.[107]

Elijah certainly appears to fit that description. He asked God to take away his life. He isolated himself from others and was staying in a cave (1 Kings 19:3, 9). He was exhausted and appeared to have lost his appetite, since he had to be told to eat (1 Kings 19:5). He was ruminating (1 Kings 19:10, 14) and thinking incorrectly. Fear of Jezebel helped bring him to this point (1 Kings 19:2), but it was also likely triggered by the failure of Israel to turn to the Lord (1 Kings 18:37). Disappointment had led to depression.

Check out *First Aid for Your Emotional Hurts: Depression.*

First Aid for Disappointment and Discouragement

Fortunately the disappointment of prophets from the past can show us the way out of disappointment and discouragement.

These things I remember, as I pour out my soul

Psalm 42:4a

Focus Your Prayers

A theme of pouring one's heart out to God emerges as we look at disappointed ministers. Just like the psalmist of Psalm 42, the prophets told God how they felt and what they thought. At times, Jeremiah's prayers were shocking. His ministry did not go as he had expected and he accused God of deceiving him (Jeremiah

20:7). He was suffering so he said he wished he had never been born (Jeremiah 20:14-15). Statements like that would result in hospitalization today. Jeremiah shows us we can tell God exactly how we feel—without fear of being accused of whining.

Jeremiah seems to have told God everything. He prayed about the anguish he felt as he watched the destruction of Judah. This would be like praying to God after a family experiences the consequences of an affair (Jeremiah 4:19-20). Jeremiah prayed to God about his pain over the spiritual immaturity of his people and the terrible sins they committed (Jeremiah 8:18-22).

We are often critical of Jonah, but he was honest and God saw fit to preserve his book for us. It shows us that we can be honest with God (He already knows); and by telling Him how disappointed we are, He can work with us to help us understand (Jonah 4:10-11).

John the Baptist coped by prayer as well. When he sent the messengers to question Jesus, that was, in effect, a prayer telling Jesus exactly how he felt and seeking answers.

> *And Jesus answered them, "Go and tell John what you hear and see: the blind receive their sight and the lame walk, lepers are cleansed and the deaf hear, and the dead are raised up, and the poor have good news preached to them.*
>
> Matthew 11:4-5

Focus on the Word

God answers us in His Word. I am always comforted by the way Jesus responded to John the Baptist. He did not tell him to stop whining, but He paraphrased some Old Testament prophecies that pointed to the Messiah (Isaiah 26, 29, 35, and 61), indirectly answering John's question by pointing him to the Word. Earlier we described how those who regularly engage in spiritual disciplines are less susceptible to burnout and more effective in ministry. Consider some of the themes in Scripture that naturally arise and aid us in the ministry. Focusing on these themes helps us cope and put our ministry in perspective.

Let us discuss a few examples. God's dealing with David shows us that the Lord looks at our heart. Often we are disappointed or hurt when people in our congregation criticize us because we are not like someone else or do not do something like a previous pastor (or worse yet, a "celebrity" pastor), or when our self-worth is tied to our church. Remember that the Lord looks at the inside (1 Samuel 16:7)—even as others look at the outside.

The scriptural teaching on contentment has been one of the most helpful passages to me (Philippians 4:11-13). It is hard to stay on track when one is low or abounding. Though we are always striving to do our best, the passage instructs us to be joyful whatever our situation (or, in our case, ministry). The Scripture also helps us to put our ministry in perspective. Rather than nitpicking the ministry of others, we are to see that everyone has a different role. It is not our job to judge them or their motives, since God uses them regardless (Philippians 1:18). The Word also helps us to put everything in perspective by seeing the big picture (Hebrews 11-12) and helping us to focus on running our own race well (Hebrews 12:1).

> *"Before I formed you in the womb I knew you,*
> *and before you were born I consecrated you;*
> *I appointed you a prophet to the nations."*
>
> Jeremiah 1:5

Focus on Your Call and Mission

When John the Baptist had doubts, Jesus was very direct with him, "Blessed is the one who is not offended by me" (Matthew 11:6). In other words, "This is the ministry I have given you—you can become offended by it or accept it." I think Jesus is saying that to many of us, when we complain to Him about how our ministry is not like some other person's ministry.

We must fulfill our ministry. I suspect as Jeremiah became discouraged, he would go back from time to time and reexamine God's call and plan for him (Jeremiah 1:4-5). Remembering the call he received and God's plan likely helped him stay on course. Has God called you? Does God have such a plan for you? Reexamine your call to the ministry and remember that the Lord goes with those He has called. When the Lord showed Jeremiah the trouble that was coming his way (Jeremiah 1:13-19), He promised Jeremiah that He would always be there for him. We too have that promise. Everyone who ministers enjoys the presence of the Lord.

> *Do you seek great things for yourself? Seek them not.*
>
> Jeremiah 45:5a

Our situation is like Jeremiah's admonition to Baruch. As you examine your call, ask yourself, "Why am I doing what I am doing?" The ministry is not the place to make a name for yourself, as Jeremiah warned Baruch. It is also not the place to seek fortune and fame. Repeatedly, we see a prerequisite to ministry is not to be a lover of money. Seeking money (and seeking fame) will lead to certain disappointment and perhaps even disaster.

> *Shepherd the flock of God that is among you, exercising oversight, not under compulsion, but willingly, as God would have you; not for shameful gain, but eagerly.*
>
> 1 Peter 5:2

Sometimes we are disappointed because our ministry is not very impressive to others. Rather than ruminating about the size of our church or our various problems, we can focus on fulfilling our ministry. Nothing good comes from feeling sorry for ourselves, but as we focus on ministry—***our ministry***—disappointment dissipates. It sounds simple, but there is no better treatment than to get busy with doing our work.

This is the same message Elijah received. After he quit his ministry, God did not give him a different ministry. He was sent right back into the ministry (1 Kings 19:15) and told to anoint Hazael as king of Syria (1 Kings 19:15), Jehu as king of Israel (1 Kings 19:16), and Elisha as a prophet (1 Kings 19:16). Long after Elijah's ministry had ended, Jehu would take care of Jezebel (2 Kings 9:30-33). Elijah had to be faithful in his ministry. We may deal with a difficult person or problem at church and see no major results from our faithfulness (our ministry). But that may lead to growth on someone else's watch decades after our ministry ends, just like Elisha and Elijah. Those changes may not happen if you are not faithful to your ministry. So let us work with the flock God has entrusted to us and, rather than seeking great things or shameful gain, may we eagerly and willingly serve.

Often in our ministry the Lord is saying, "Not yet." Moses appeared to have been poised to deliver Israel from Egypt (Exodus 2) when God apparently said, "Not yet." Eventually God did call him to fulfill a ministry of delivering Israel from Egypt (Exodus 3). If we will continue on in doing well, we may later see church growth and the kind of ministry we long for. But if not, let us be faithful and content.

> *. . . the devil. . . is a liar and the father of lies.*
>
> John 8:44

Focus on Your Thinking

The devil wants to discourage you, and he is very good at it since he is the father of lies. One way he discourages is by making things seem worse than they really are. To combat his traps, we again think about how we must be sober. It is a way of taking control of your thinking, a refusal to think wrong thoughts. When disappointment sets in, it can begin to impact how we view everything, and it can hamper our ministry. When faced with disappointment, it is important that our thinking is correct.

> "Don't let the disappointment in a few sheep keep you from loving the many."
>
> **Jeana Floyd**

> *. . . An overseer must be . . . soberminded . . .*
>
> 1 Timothy 3:2a-3a

As stated in the Jeana Floyd quote above, we do not want disappointment to rob us of loving others.[108] We must determine the true nature of a situation. Do not exaggerate the difficulty, but do not minimize or ignore the difficulty either. For example, a common comment heard in the ministry that can lead to disappointment and discouragement is, "people are saying." To look at this statement soberly one might ask, "Which people?" Are these people very influential? Are these people who always complain? Does "people" equate to 20, 10, or just 1 (the person doing the reporting)? Rather than jumping to a conclusion that one has fallen out of favor with half of the congregation, we must think with sober judgment, which can keep our disappointment in check. An example of this kind of situation is the threat Elijah received from Jezebel (1 Kings 19:2). Elijah failed to soberly examine the situation and overstated the problem saying everyone was trying to kill him (1 Kings 19:10, 14). The Lord helped him reassess the situation by looking soberly at the real situation, noting 7,000 people had not bowed to Baal, which was the correct assessment (1 Kings 19:18).

Part of Elijah's problem was that he saw his situation as being worse than it really was. We, too, do this in a variety of ways. We often compound disappointment and discouragement by comparing our situation to that of others. We think someone else has a better ministry than us or compare ourselves to a larger more visible ministry.

As for you, always be sober-minded, endure suffering, do the work of an evangelist, fulfill your ministry.
2 Timothy 4:5

What do you do when someone leaves your church? Put the disappointment in perspective by asking yourself a series of questions.

What percentage of this was my fault?

What can I learn from this situation?

When do I implement the Saul principle?

The Lord said to Samuel, "How long will you grieve over Saul..."
1 Samuel 16:1a

Mourn and Move On

Perhaps the hardest disappointment to cope with is when people leave the church or fall into sin. There is no escaping it; this leads to disappointment, and it is fine to grieve the setback for a period, but not to the point where it begins to impact our ministry to others. David mourned the loss of Absalom after he was defeated and killed trying to take over the kingdom. After seeing his mourning over the event and its impact upon his soldiers, Joab reprimanded David (2 Samuel 19:1-8). For us this would be like mourning over someone who has left the church at the expense of those who stayed. Second guessing ourselves with questions like, "What if I had done . . ." can be dangerous if it goes on too long. We want to soberly examine situations and get focused on ministry.

Sometimes God demands that we move on. There is a point where God tells Jeremiah not to pray for certain people (Jeremiah 7:16-20). Similarly, Samuel mourned the failure of Saul for some time until God confronted him (1 Samuel 16:1). God's instruction to Samuel was to move his focus from Saul to David. Consider the quote below.[109]

> Rather than focus on your disappointment look for an opportunity to honor and commend others.
> **Jeana Floyd**

When we continue to think about the disappointment from a setback we become especially vulnerable to attack from the devil (1 Peter 5:8-9). In some ways, when we push back on disappointment we are resisting the devil. We can do this by celebrating those who serve well rather than concentrating on those who disappoint.

> *Therefore an overseer must be . . . self-controlled . . . not violent but gentle, not quarrelsome . . .*
> 1 Timothy 3:2a, 3a

Threat: Complaining, Criticism, and Sabotage

One of my first observations upon entering the pastorate was that people complain a lot. People complain about the music (too loud, not loud enough, not to mention the genre), about activities (too many, not enough, the time and duration), facilities (upkeep, cost of upkeep), and about everything else. People complain about us. Our messages are too long or short—actually the latter is pretty rare. We did not visit them or we did—again, the latter is rare though it does happen. I even had someone complain about my haircut once—too short.

Complaining is one thing, but criticism is another; and of course the worst is when someone actually tries to sabotage your ministry. Though we may be shocked by this, we should not be. The prerequisites to being a pastor suggest this kind of environment. The pastor must have self-control so they can't be perturbed and strike back when criticized. It is hard to know what to do sometimes, especially when someone attacks you. We are not like a politician who hits back, we are followers of Jesus. We must be gentle. Further, the pastor cannot be quarrelsome. There will be plenty of people who would like to fight. If the pastor is quick to engage them, it is a recipe for his demise. We must possess and embrace these characteristics or we will fall into disgrace, which is the devil's trap. Sometimes I think social media has contributed to our current environment of criticizing and complaining, where people often speak without a filter and find it easier to be critical when not interacting with another person face to face. It may seem like the atmosphere is pretty bad today, but Moses might disagree with us about it being worse. We can learn a lot about unpleasantness in ministry by examining the challenges he endured.

Moses Knows Complaining

And the people grumbled against Moses, saying, "What shall we drink?"

Exodus 15:24

But the people thirsted there for water, and the people grumbled against Moses and said, "Why did you bring us up out of Egypt, to kill us and our children and our livestock with thirst?"

Exodus 17:3

(continued on next page)

And the whole congregation of the people of Israel grumbled against Moses and Aaron in the wilderness.

Exodus 16:2

And all the people of Israel grumbled against Moses and Aaron. The whole congregation said to them, "Would that we had died in the land of Egypt! Or would that we had died in this wilderness!

Numbers 14:2

. . . you would not go up, but rebelled against the command of the Lord your God. And you murmured in your tents . . .

Deuteronomy 1:26-27a

Complaining

Moses certainly knew what it was like to hear complaining. Things did not go well as Israel began to prepare to leave Egypt. The words Moses heard were stinging. Interestingly, people complained to him about many things over which he really had no control. Sometimes it can seem like it is all the pastor's fault. Often people complain about something you cannot do anything about, like the slow progress on a building project or someone leaving the church.

Moses Knows Criticism

They said to Moses, "Is it because there are no graves in Egypt that you have taken us away to die in the wilderness? What have you done to us in bringing us out of Egypt?

Exodus 14:11

"The Lord look on you and judge, because you have made us stink in the sight of Pharaoh and his servants, and have put a sword in their hand to kill us."

Exodus 5:21

Criticism

People can be very critical. Sometimes people exaggerate the good old days. In Exodus 16, the Israelites made it sound like they reclined at a pool while pots of meat were brought to them.

They seem to have forgotten they were slaves. This is like embarking on a new ministry or a ministry shift while many are complaining to you about the initial hiccups. Just before Israel was liberated from the Egyptians all appeared to be pretty bleak, and Israel complained to Moses. This would be akin to providing biblical counseling to a family and their initial response being unfavorable.

Then there are the times when someone is just critical. Sometimes there is no logic to it. There will be people who do not like you and will not like you no matter what you do. When I first began to pastor, someone told me a person (who I had never met) was ill and in the hospital (two counties away). She suggested I visit the person saying, "Maybe you could turn an enemy into a friend." I did not know these people. I had never met them. How could they be an enemy?

Moses Knows Attack and Sabotage

Miriam and Aaron spoke against Moses because of the Cushite woman whom he had married, for he had married a Cushite woman. And they said, "Has the Lord indeed spoken only through Moses? Has he not spoken through us also?"

Numbers 12:1-2a

They assembled themselves together against Moses and against Aaron and said to them, "You have gone too far! For all in the congregation are holy, every one of them, and the Lord is among them. Why then do you exalt yourselves above the assembly of the Lord?"

Numbers 16:3

Now there was no water for the congregation. And they assembled themselves together against Moses and against Aaron. And the people quarreled with Moses and said, "Would that we had perished when our brothers perished before the Lord!

Numbers 20:2-3

And the people spoke against God and against Moses, "Why have you brought us up out of Egypt to die in the wilderness? For there is no food and no water, and we loathe this worthless food."

Numbers 21:5

Attacks and Sabotage

The complaining and criticism against Moses escalated to attacks. The attack recorded in Numbers 20 is where Moses failed to handle the situation well and struck the rock. That event came right after the death of his sister Miriam. Moses was especially vulnerable and if there ever were a time for cooperation, that was the time.

Some people will try to sabotage the work of the church. Sometimes you can clearly identify them. At other times you will be surprised (even Miriam and Aaron once attacked Moses). However, the quicker you are able to identify what is really going on, the better your position to address it.

> *For Demas, in love with this present world, has deserted me and gone to Thessalonica. Crescens has gone to Galatia, Titus to Dalmatia.*
>
> 2 Timothy 4:10

First, it is important to recognize that there are some people who attack pastors. Lloyd Rediger has written extensively about people who inflict harm upon pastors and the church, whom he refers to as clergy killers.

> *For they cannot sleep unless they have done wrong; they are robbed of sleep unless they have made someone stumble.*
>
> Proverbs 4:16

The first characteristic of clergy killers is they are destructive. They don't just disagree or criticize, they insist on inflicting pain and damaging their targets. They may engage in sabotage, subvert worthy causes, and incite others to do their dirty work, causing victims to self-destruct.[110] This is what happened to Moses when he struck the rock. They are those of whom the Proverbs speak who cannot sleep unless they make someone stumble. They are adept at sowing discord among the brothers (Proverbs 6:19).

> *Those who seek my life lay their snares;*
> *those who seek my hurt speak of ruin*
> *and meditate treachery all day long.*
>
> Psalm 38:12

They are determined, and always thinking of what they can do to create difficulty. They may pause or change tactics, but they intimidate, network, and break rules of decency to accomplish destruction. Their agenda is their priority.

> *A false witness who breathes out lies,*
> *and one who sows discord among brothers.*
>
> Proverbs 6:19

They are deceitful. They manipulate, misrepresent, and accuse others of their own tactics. Their statements and negotiations are not trustworthy.

> *And Saul eyed David from that day on. The next day a harmful spirit from God rushed upon Saul, and he raved within his house while David was playing the lyre, as he did day by day. Saul had his spear in his hand. And Saul hurled the spear, for he thought, "I will pin David to the wall." But David evaded him twice.*
>
> 1 Samuel 18:9-11

They may be evil or mentally ill. A pastor may become a symbol or scapegoat for their own internal pain or spiritual confusion, as was the case with David as he dealt with Saul. I am a trained mental health counselor and I acknowledge it is sometimes hard to determine whether the actions of others are the result of mental illness or evil. Regardless of the source of the problem, they are disruptive.

The church tends to be in denial about clergy killers, and in this way people often collude with them. Most do not want to admit, acknowledge, or believe someone would cause this kind of intentional damage. Often they point to how these people have helped in other ways. This leaves clergy killers unrestrained and the pastor and the church vulnerable.[111]

> "The only thing required for the triumph of evil is for good men to do nothing."
> **Edmund Burke**

The individuals that Rediger described as clergy killers are also church killers. One of the reasons they thrive, according to Rediger, is that no one wants to believe someone would have those motives. In my experience, many people flee a church once they get a sense that they may be in a church with someone like this. I have a hypothesis that these people prey on smaller churches where they are able to manipulate a few people to get their way. As people flee a church, it becomes increasingly more difficult to find people to combat the clergy killer. In larger churches, except in a small group setting, the attacks of a clergy killer are less effective.

Discernment is the prescription for dealing with these people, who are masters of disguise when they choose to be.[112] Take a moment to assess where you are as you encounter complaining and criticism.[113]

Is This True of You?

I frequently have conflict with a church member or staff member

←---→

Rarely true — Almost always true

I can depend upon the support of my deacon/elder board in times of conflict

←---→

Rarely true — Almost always true

I am criticized personally by someone in a leadership role in the congregation

←---→

Rarely true — Almost always true

I am criticized face-to-face by a member

←---→

Rarely true — Almost always true

A ministry decision was made that affected me and my family, but I was not consulted

←---→

Rarely true | Almost always true

A member complained to me about someone in my family

←---→

Rarely true | Almost always true

Indeed, all who desire to live a godly life in Christ Jesus will be persecuted.

2 Timothy 3:12

First Aid for Complaining, Criticism, and Sabotage

As a minister, our goal must be to do our best to be a small target for criticism. A prerequisite to the ministry is to be above reproach, which will reduce legitimate criticism. Our goal is to uphold, withstand, and even use these negative events to propel the ministry. Let us go ahead and look at some guidelines when it comes to complaining, criticism, and sabotage.

Keep your heart with all vigilance,
for from it flow the springs of life.
Put away from you crooked speech,
and put devious talk far from you.
Let your eyes look directly forward,
and your gaze be straight before you.
Ponder the path of your feet;
then all your ways will be sure.
Do not swerve to the right or to the left;
turn your foot away from evil.

Proverbs 4:23-27

Don't Let Bitterness Overtake You

Do not allow complaining, criticism, and sabotage to derail your ministry. To guard against that, refuse to allow bitterness to grow in your heart. That means we will have to pray a lot (more on that later), and be very careful about what we say when dealing with complaints. The goal of the devil is that we will get off of our mission, so we want to stay focused on our ministry, and be careful about our own actions lest we act out in anger and begin harming others as well.

> *He said to them, "An enemy has done this." So the servants said to him, "Then do you want us to go and gather them?" But he said, "No, lest in gathering the weeds you root up the wheat along with them."*
>
> Matthew 13:28-29

This seems to be what Jesus is getting at with the parable of the sower in Matthew 13 and the dealing with weeds. If we are not very careful in our handling of these issues we will harm innocent people. If we will be patient, the Lord will eventually sort it out.

> *Refrain from anger, and forsake wrath!*
> *Fret not yourself; it tends only to evil.*
>
> Psalm 37:8

We cannot let conflict overtake us and dominate our thoughts. This is a fine line to walk. We must address these problems, yet we cannot constantly think about them or they will render us ineffective in the ministry. Finally, do not quit over complaining and conflict. Too many pastors flee at the first sign of trouble. I promise you that you will find it at the next church too. Our best bet is to anticipate complaining, criticism, and even a few saboteurs, and prepare to deal with them. Let us begin by anticipating criticism.

Do: Anticipate Complaining and Criticism

There has always been complaining in the church (Acts 6:1). People complained about the apostles. They also complained about Stephen who was doing well. They rose up against him (Acts 6:9), and even when he did not lash out at them (Acts 6:15) and only tried to help them (Acts 7), they destroyed him.

> You know they crucified Jesus and He was perfect.
> **J. P. Seley**

Once I was complaining to a faithful deacon, J. P. Seley, about some criticism I received. Over the course of the conversation, he reminded me that they criticized and crucified Jesus. He was right, and the implication was that as ministers of the gospel we, too, can expect criticism. They criticized Jesus because they wanted to see a sign (Matthew 12:38; Mark 8:11-12) even though He had performed many miracles. They tried to trap Him in questions about divorce (Matthew 19:3-9) and about taxes (Matthew 22:15-22). They spied on Him (Luke 20:20-26). They criticized Him for ministering to people who were too sinful (Luke 7:36-39). They conspired against Him to destroy Him (Matthew 12:14). What more can we expect?

As a rule, anything worthwhile will be criticized. A good example is the building of the Brooklyn Bridge. I was able to visit the Brooklyn Bridge after reading David McCullough's book *The Great Bridge*. The Roebling family sacrificed dearly to build the bridge. The patriarch, John Roebling's foot was crushed in the early work on the bridge. As a result, he developed tetanus and eventually died from the injury. His son, Washington Roebling, took over the task, which would eventually take 14 years to complete. Though he was unaware of it at the time, Washington Roebling developed the bends as the bridge was being built. His health was never the same. Yet he persisted, and his remarkable dedication and engineering skills resulted in the incredible bridge. There was nothing like it at the time and it was noted for its architectural beauty and practicality. The bridge builder had many critics though. In 1882, the *New York Star* wrote, "The best way to secure the rapid and effective work is to get a new Chief Engineer." Near the end of the project, a vote of confidence was held by the board overseeing the building of the bridge. Roebling was only able to keep his job by one vote. Anything worthwhile will have opposition. The bridge was worthwhile. It changed New York City. Even today, an average 112,000 vehicles cross the bridge daily. Later in life, Roebling was asked how he was able to carry on. He replied, ". . . it's my job to carry the responsibility, and you can't desert your job. You can't slink out of life or out of the work life lays on you."[114] Let us not slink from our work over a little criticism. Let us expect it and keep going.

> *Do not take to heart all the things that people say,*
> *lest you hear your servant cursing you.*
> Ecclesiastes 7:21

Do: Put Criticism in Perspective

Since people do tend to complain about everything, they often do not really mean some of the things they say. That is the teaching from the book of Ecclesiastes. Perhaps we should rephrase it for ministry, "Do not take to heart all the things people say, lest you hear your parishioner criticizing you." It is a bit like the way people complain about the government or even traffic. People really do not mean harm; they are just going to complain.

Further, they often do not know what they are doing to you or the church. So it is better if we avoid thinking about many of the complaints unless it is helpful. Let us acknowledge, though, that a lot of criticism is helpful. So rather, than getting upset we should ask questions about it. Sometimes criticism is actually feedback or helpful accountability.

When criticized, ask yourself . . .

Is it warranted?

Is it legitimate?

Is it loyal?

Is it vindictive?

Does an action need to be taken?

We need to know when something is awry, and criticism is a good way to address that. Quickly, you should be able to get a sense as to whether something is feedback or constructive criticism. The destructive person is never satisfied, and is uninterested in improvement. As we minister, we more clearly understand the difference between legitimate and illegitimate criticism. I believe a key to this is prayer. Clergy killers are rare, so most of the conflicts we deal with are innocuous complaints and opportunities for improvement. It is important to ask ourselves as we deal with people whether the conflict (or criticism) is over a preference or a principle, which can often help us as we strive for unity.

"I take it to God in prayer. I don't quarrel with the members."
"What I know is that we're here because of
the Lord. There's nothing else."

Do: Pray

The pastors quoted above described praying to address criticism and conflict.[115] No matter what, we need to talk to the Lord when we are hurt by the things people say. Repeatedly, Moses went to the Lord after people complained to him or attacked him

(Exodus 5:22, 14:15, 15:25, 17:4, Numbers 12:4, 14:13). Moses prayed a lot, and no doubt this sustained him. He also prayed for those who persecuted him (Exodus 32:30-35, Deuteronomy 9:13-14). Those prayers likely helped Moses to love them as Jesus would later instruct us to do.

> *Love your enemies and pray for those who persecute you*
>
> Matthew 5:44b

As we pray for them, I think we become better at helping them and identifying their real problem. Then, over the course of time, God fixes a lot of problems through circumstances or moving in the heart of the critic.

Prayer helps us minister. Earlier I quoted J. P. Seley, a man who was such an encouragement to me in the ministry. He died at the age of 94. Though he lived a good life and I was not surprised by his death, I was quite upset as I prepared to conduct his funeral. About three hours before his funeral I received one of the most critical emails I have ever received in the ministry. Actually, the email felt a bit threatening. It was the kind of email that could ruin your day—even your week. Now I believe the one who sent the email was mentally ill, but I also think the timing of the email was out of the evil one's playbook. I thought of the time that Hezekiah received a bad letter from the king of Assyria and laid it out before the Lord.

> *Hezekiah received the letter from the hand of the messengers, and read it; and Hezekiah went up to the house of the Lord, and spread it before the Lord.*
>
> Isaiah 37:14

I laid the printed email out before the Lord and gave it to Him. Doing so enabled me to focus completely on the funeral. I think we need to lay out many things before the Lord. Personally, that enables me to put many problems aside and keep them from growing into a major problem.

For I hear the whispering of many—
terror on every side!—
as they scheme together against me,
as they plot to take my life.
But I trust in you, O Lord;
I say, "You are my God."
Psalm 31:13-14

Perhaps there is nothing more painful than to pour your life into someone, pray for them, worry for them, and then see them turn on you and actually try to inflict harm upon you.

My soul is in the midst of lions;
I lie down amid fiery beasts—
the children of man, whose teeth are spears and arrows,
whose tongues are sharp swords.
Psalm 57:4

How are we to pray about situations where we encounter clergy killers? When people oppressed Jeremiah, he talked to the Lord and asked Him to deal with those people (Jeremiah 11:19-23; 12:1-6). Jeremiah told God how displeased he was after the persecution he received from Pashur (Jeremiah 20). We can do this as well. Consider Psalm 143 below.

A Prayer for Being Attacked

Hear my prayer, O Lord; give ear to my pleas for mercy!...
For the enemy has pursued my soul; he has crushed my life to the ground; he has made me sit in darkness like those long dead.
Therefore my spirit faints within me;
my heart within me is appalled.
I remember the days of old;
I meditate on all that you have done; I ponder the work of your hands.
I stretch out my hands to you;

my soul thirsts for you like a parched land. Selah
Answer me quickly, O Lord!
My spirit fails!
Hide not your face from me,
lest I be like those who go down to the pit.
Let me hear in the morning of your steadfast love,
for in you I trust.
Make me know the way I should go,
for to you I lift up my soul.
Deliver me from my enemies, O Lord!
I have fled to you for refuge.
Teach me to do your will,
for you are my God!
Let your good Spirit lead me
on level ground!
For your name's sake, O Lord, preserve my life!
In your righteousness bring my soul out of trouble!
And in your steadfast love you will cut off my enemies,
and you will destroy all the adversaries of my soul,
for I am your servant.

Psalm 143

There are several Psalms you can pray in these situations. Psalm 35 is a good prayer for dealing with contention. The psalmist asks God to contend for him and defend him (Psalm 35:1-4). He talks about how people had maliciously attacked him and done evil to him after he had done good to them (Psalm 35:11-13), and prayed for God to rescue him.

In Psalm 43 the psalmist prays for vindication against those who are ungodly (Psalm 43:1), and that God's light and truth would go out (Psalm 43:3), and for him to be able to worship with exceeding joy (Psalm 43:4). He seems to talk back to himself, asking himself why he is cast down, and acknowledging he will praise God again (Psalm 43:5).

In Psalm 55 the Psalmist asks God to help him (Psalm 55:1-3) and describes the pain he experiences as a result of attacks upon him (Psalm 55:4-5). He longs to just leave or fly away (Psalm 55:6-8). He directly asks for their tongues to be destroyed and notes the violence they cause (Psalm 55:9-10). After discussing some of the damage they cause (Psalm 55:11-12), he notes that this person was once his friend and they worshiped together (Psalm 55:13-20). He also notes that the person who has turned against him uses "smooth" speech (Psalm 55:21).

Over the years there has been a lot of debate about Rediger's clergy killer concept. Some have not liked his characterization of those he describes.[116] However, a perusal of the Scripture indicates that there will be some occasions where people are bent on inflicting harm upon the work of God—otherwise, there would be no need for many of these Psalms. As we pray, the Lord will often make it clear that we must take action.

> *For there are many who are insubordinate, empty talkers and deceivers, especially those of the circumcision party. They must be silenced, since they are upsetting whole families by teaching for shameful gain what they ought not to teach.*
>
> Titus 1:10-11

Do: Confront and Deal With Sin

In Titus 1, Paul says that those who are insubordinate and empty talkers must be stopped. This is the job of the church leader. Paul is making it clear that there will be times when we will need to ask a board member to step down lest they infect the whole church (1 Corinthians 5:5-7). Paul more thoroughly described what he was referring to in Romans 16.

> *I appeal to you, brothers, to watch out for those who cause divisions and create obstacles contrary to the doctrine that you have been taught; avoid them. For such persons do not serve our Lord Christ, but their own appetites, and by smooth talk and flattery they deceive the hearts of the naive. For your obedience is known to all, so that I rejoice over you, but I want you to be wise as to what is good and innocent as to what is evil. The God of peace will soon crush Satan under your feet. The grace of our Lord Jesus Christ be with you.*
>
> Romans 16:17-20

There is no denying this is very difficult work, but it is necessary. None of us dreamed of doing the things required to address this kind of sin. I love the movie *Saving Private Ryan,* and it contains a scene that describes this phenomenon.

The unit comes upon a German machine gun nest. In the background you can see the bodies of American soldiers who have been victims of the German encampment. The men suggest they go around the Germans and continue with their mission to find Private Ryan. Captain Miller points out their greater mission of winning the war and notes that if they go around the encampment they will be leaving the problem for future allied soldiers who will likely face certain death. He orders his men to engage the machine gun nest. They successfully take the nest out but lose their medic in the process. As I have watched this scene, I could not help but be reminded of the bullies in many churches who desperately need church discipline, but instead they are left for the next pastor to address.

As we discuss dealing with these problems, other leaders or even family members may suggest it is best for us to let it go and perhaps easiest in the short run. However, we are trying to win a spiritual war, and it is important that we consider the eternal consequences of failing to act. A good example is the case of Hezekiah.

> *Behold, the days are coming, when all that is in your house, and that which your fathers have stored up till this day, shall be carried to Babylon. Nothing shall be left, says the Lord. And some of your own sons, who will come from you, whom you will father, shall be taken away, and they shall be eunuchs in the palace of the king of Babylon." Then Hezekiah said to Isaiah, "The word of the Lord that you have spoken is good." For he thought, "Why not, if there will be peace and security in my days?"*
>
> 2 Kings 20:17-19

Hezekiah did not take the long view of the ministry. He created problems for which future generations paid dearly. He was unconcerned because he personally did not experience this difficulty. As a minister, be concerned about what follows you. Sometimes we fight battles for those who may not even be at the church yet, or even for a future pastor who may never know what we have sacrificed so that they may have success.

> *And if anyone will not receive you or listen to your words, shake off the dust from your feet when you leave that house or town.*
>
> Matthew 10:14

Do: Stay on Offense

Jesus was pretty clear that when you are rejected by others that you are to take the message or invest in those who will receive the message. He was attacked by the religious leaders, so He went to the tax collectors and harlots. Paul was criticized by the Jews, so he took the gospel to the Gentiles. Stay on offense. Pour yourself into study and preaching and those in need.

> *As for you, you meant evil against me, but God meant it for good, to bring it about that many people should be kept alive, as they are today.*
>
> Genesis 50:20

You can stay on offense because no matter what happens, you will win. Even when they hurt you or even when they defeat you, you win. That is the teaching of Romans 8:28 as well as what Joseph shared in Genesis 50. The selling of Joseph into slavery (Genesis 37) was terrible, but God used it. It was the kind of thing that could make one bitter—drive some out of the ministry. Joseph did not sweep what happened under a rug or ignore it. The names of his children reflect the pain and difficulty he experienced (Genesis 41:51-52) at that time. He also dealt with the offense as he tested his brothers (Genesis 42-45) when they came to Egypt. Yet, this mistreatment made Joseph into a better person. This kind of adversity will make us better ministers. Hang in there and keep ministering.

> *He said to him the third time, "Simon, son of John, do you love me?" Peter was grieved because he said to him the third time, "Do you love me?" and he said to him, "Lord, you know everything; you know that I love you." Jesus said to him, "Feed my sheep.*
>
> John 21:17

Threats to Ministers: Failure

We fail a lot. We have already seen how 8 out of 10 churches in the U.S. are not growing. We in the ministry fail in many ways. We also fail personally. For example, one in five pastors reports struggling at some time with an addiction, most commonly pornography.[117]

Everyone who ministers will know failure, and will feel, at times, that they do not know what they are doing. Some of what happens in the ministry can result in feelings of inadequacy. Jeremiah felt that way, as can be seen when he said, "I am only a youth" (Jeremiah 1:6), and no doubt as has already been described when Judah fell to Babylon. So did Elijah as Ahab and Israel failed to respond to his message, and John the Baptist as he was rejected and placed in a prison.

When I read about the life of Moses it reminds me of some of the challenges of ministry. Consider Moses' defense of an Israelite man (Exodus 2). It appears he was ready to help his people push back on Egyptian oppression, but they were not yet ready to move forward (Acts 7:25). His timing was off by about 40 years. We have all been there. You had a great ministry idea, but got shot down. This explains Moses' initial response at the fiery bush, "Lord please send someone else" (Exodus 4:13). He was reluctant to go through the pain of a possible rejection again. Then he found that the task took much longer than it needed to have taken. Moses could easily have felt like a failure, as he was unable to get the first generation of Israelites, or himself, into the promised land.

When I think of leaders who failed, one who comes to my mind is Peter. Peter certainly knew failure. He walked on water and then he literally fell (Matthew 14:28-30). At the transfiguration he said the wrong thing (Luke 9). When asked about a tax, he spoke too soon (Matthew 17:24-27). We may think we are a failure, but has anyone ever referred to us as Satan? Jesus referred to Peter as Satan as he was hindering His focus upon the cross (Matthew 16:23). Peter fell asleep in Gethsemane (Mark 14:32-37) when Jesus needed him the most. He did the wrong thing when he cut off the ear of a solider (John 18:10-11), and let Jesus down again by denying Him three times (John 18:15-27). A man who was not even a believer during this period would later need to confront Peter when he failed to treat Gentiles fairly (Galatians 2:11-14). But after each failure, Peter learned, and he grew. He answered the call into ministry (John 21), and we have all been blessed for it. God turns failure into success. God uses imperfect people. Do you feel like a failure? Consider and respond to the statements below.

I wish I were in some other vocation

←---→

Rarely true — Almost always true

I feel my fellow ministers respect and appreciate my vocational efforts

←---→

Rarely true — Almost always true

> *For by the grace given to me I say to everyone among you not to think of himself more highly than he ought to think, but to think with sober judgment, each according to the measure of faith that God has assigned.*
>
> Romans 12:3

First Aid for Failure

Overcoming failure can make us more resilient and more effective in what we do if we approach failure the right way. The key is that we think soberly about each situation. We all do not have the same opportunities or the same abilities. All the Lord asks of us is that we faithfully fulfill the tasks He has laid before us. Jesus taught us in the parable of the talents (Luke 19:12-27) that we will be held accountable for how we use our opportunities, abilities, and spend our time.

Think Soberly

About Your Strengths and Weaknesses

Let us begin by asking ourselves whether we are properly utilizing our gifts. In his discussion on spiritual gifts, Paul instructed us "to think with sober judgment" (Romans 12:3). In other words, conduct an honest self-assessment about what you are good at. Determine what your real gifts are, and use those gifts heavily. Do not inflate or deflate your capabilities in a particular area, and do not try to be someone else. So what are you good at? What are you not as good at? The God who called you has people who need your particular gifts to minister effectively to them, so develop into the person you have been made to be. There are people attracted to you regardless of your style and gifts.[118]

About Your Failures

When you do fail, learn from it. In Rainer's research on breakout churches, the people they referred to as Acts 6-7 leaders never viewed a setback as a failure.[119] Some have described failures or setbacks as experiments that did not work. We can learn from every situation. When something does not go well ask yourself, "What went wrong? How can I improve? What might I do differently?" Slow progress is fine as long as you are progressing. If we face a setback, can we implement change differently and have a different result?

Rather than getting bogged down by embarrassment or even shame about a setback, we might take Luther's advice to "sin boldly that grace may abound." Luther was not actually saying we should sin, but that we should keep trying rather than engaging in a paralysis of analysis. God in His grace forgives us and uses our feeble attempts to serve Him.[120]

> *But I discipline my body and keep it under control, lest after preaching to others I myself should be disqualified.*
>
> 1 Corinthians 9:27

About Accountability

We need to think soberly about accountability. I believe there is little accountability in most churches. That places us at risk for both moral failure and loss of effectiveness in the ministry. Because there is so much criticism and conflict, we may begin to wish that everyone would just leave us alone without much oversight. However, scrutiny is valuable. What if Paul had left Peter alone when he refused to treat Gentiles appropriately (Galatians 2:11-13)? That would have been bad for the church and for Peter. Several years ago, I watched an interview on the Gospel Coalition with three well-known pastors. Two of them seemed a bit arrogant and, I assumed, would be immune to much of the second guessing and criticism the average pastor endures. Today, those two pastors have been removed from their positions by their church leadership. Oversight is not so bad after all, especially if it helps us stay on track. To truly succeed, we need accountability to help prevent us from being disqualified in the ministry.

> "It is a sin to be good if God has called you to be great."
> **Thom Rainer**

About Your Work

In Rainer's research on churches, he found that when something went wrong breakout pastors were quick to accept responsibility. They also had a strong emphasis upon excellence.[121] The nature of the ministry often results in people not truly knowing what we are doing. For example, you can be in your study but not really studying. The ministry is a place where one can slide into mediocrity easily. Too often, I fear we in the ministry begin to think it is not important to strive for excellence. This is a sin. We are doing the most important work in the world. Let us do it well, even if only Jesus will be the one who sees it.

> We first make our habits, and then our habits make us.
> **John Dryden**

The way we do our work begins to define us as habits are formed. We want to work excellently habitually. As you develop your habits you need to know yourself well and how you work best.

> *Do you not know that in a race all the runners run, but only one receives the prize? So run that you may obtain it. Every athlete exercises self-control in all things. They do it to receive a perishable wreath, but we an imperishable. So I do not run aimlessly; I do not box as one beating the air. But I discipline my body and keep it under control, lest after preaching to others I myself should be disqualified.*
>
> 1 Corinthians 9:24-27

About How You Do Your Work

Part of working with excellence is to know when you do your best work. The time at which you do things matters. This has especially been documented with medical procedures. For example, physicians find more abnormalities when conducting colonoscopies in the morning than in the afternoon, because most physicians do their best work in the morning. All of us have moods that rise and fall throughout the day. This can even be seen in research on Twitter posts. The average Twitter user has a happiness spike around breakfast, they hit a grumpy slump in later afternoon, and perk up again after dinner.[122] In another study, financial executives were upbeat in the morning and more negative as the day went on.[123] Should you avoid working in the afternoon? It is not that simple.

> *So teach us to number our days*
> *that we may get a heart of wisdom.*
>
> Psalm 90:12

Although there are overall trends as to when people do their best work, everyone is different. There are strong morning types, moderate morning types, strong evening types, moderate evening types, and even neutral types that (peak at midday). Which type are you?

You probably know intuitively what type you are. Our daily patterns are more than mere preferences. They are referred to as a chronotype, which is a biological characteristic. Your chronotype is not permanent. As we age, our circadian rhythmicity shifts. In older age, we slide more toward preferring morning hours but our variation is what determines our peak period and maximum performance period. This has major implications for when you do your best work. You are better off doing difficult mental chores at a time consistent with your chronotype. If you are a morning person, you do not want to spend your time in the beginning of the morning going through your email. You would be more effective doing deep work like sermon preparation. A better time to do mundane work would be the afternoon. If you are trying to do something creative, like come up with an illustration, you might revisit that during an off-peak coffee break. If you are working on a task where you need to be creative, it is actually more helpful to engage in that activity during a period that is not at your nonoptimal time. Often people ask if they can change their chronotype. You can alter your rhythms by the use of light. For example, exposing yourself to bright light in the evening can push your circadian patterns later into the evening. However, remember that it is hard to work against your biology.[124]

It is important that we do our best work and be energized by our work. As a whole that happens for pastors. Look below at how energized pastors are in their work when compared to the general population.[125]

Energized by Work

	Frequently	Sometimes	Seldom/Never
Pastors	60%	37%	4%
General Population	24%	38%	38%

It is important to work well, but we must also engage in the correct work.

What is the Pastor Called to Do?

Shepherd the flock of God that is among you, exercising oversight, not under compulsion, but willingly, as God would have you; not for shameful gain, but eagerly.

1 Peter 5:2

Preach the word; be ready in season and out of season; reprove, rebuke, and exhort, with complete patience and teaching.

2 Timothy 4:2

Therefore an overseer must be . . . able to teach.

1 Timothy 3:2

He must hold firm to the trustworthy word as taught, so that he may be able to give instruction in sound doctrine and also to rebuke those who contradict it.

Titus 1:9

Do What You Were Called to Do

Soberly examine how you spend your time. Though it would have been service, waiting on tables was the wrong thing for the apostles to do (Acts 6:2). To succeed in the ministry we need to devote a significant amount of our time to doing what the Scripture says pastors are to do. What does the Scripture indicate we need to focus upon? Our primary task is shepherding and exercising oversight, and preaching and teaching the Word.

Therefore, the critical and key requirements that must be our primary focus are discipling, training, planning, and protecting the flock from divisions. Further, since "able to teach" is a specific requirement of the pastor, we must make this a major priority.

Spend time preparing to preach and honing your preaching skills. You can work all day, but if it is on the wrong thing you will be wasting your time. Our motto must be to make the best use of our time. So how are you doing? Take the survey on the next page from Faucett, Corwyn, and Poling.[126]

I am satisfied that my job utilizes my training and capabilities

←---→

Rarely true Almost always true

I find meaning and purpose in my work

←---→

Rarely true Almost always true

I feel I am doing the work God wants me to do

←---→

Rarely true Almost always true

If we find ourselves doing many tasks that do not meet scriptural criteria, it is important to find others to fulfill these tasks. We struggled early in my ministry to find people to perform these tasks, so we recruited the youth. In addition to getting the tasks completed, this provided opportunities for us to train and mentor these youth, most of whom are still ministering in churches today.

We want to make sure our service fulfills our responsibility of shepherding the flock and exercising oversight. It is helpful to ask, "Does this activity enable me to shepherd the flock of God?" To shepherd a flock is to feed, protect, and nourish. Since there is so much to do, it is important to evaluate the tasks we are engaged in and ask whether we should be doing them.

Should I be engaging in this task?

What is the cost?

How much time is it taking?

What am I not doing so that I can complete this task?

What is the benefit?

Does it meet the scripturally prescribed duty for pastors?

Does the benefit outweigh the cost?

Who could I train to perform this task?

Consider going through this process as you contemplate engaging in a task. Today there are many expectations regarding pastors and visiting. Use visiting the sick as a ministry, but be careful that it not take the place of key tasks pastors are called to perform. I often think of Jesus' words about the poor in this area.

> *For you always have the poor with you, and whenever you want, you can do good for them. But you will not always have me.*
>
> Mark 14:7

There will always be needy people or situations we are unable to fix. In the context of this passage, Jesus was saying the presence of needy people would not interfere with His time with the Father. Pressing needs cannot keep us from time with the Lord or time for shepherding and preparing to preach. We must use our time on those things we have been called to do. Incidentally, in *Breakout Churches*, Rainer and his team found that breakout church leaders put significant emphasis on excellence in preaching, specifically study and message preparation. They also gave away many non-ministry tasks to laypeople, which allowed them to spend more time on critical ministries while allowing the church to develop strong lay ministries.[127]

> *When you come, bring the cloak that I left with Carpus at Troas, also the books, and above all the parchments.*
>
> 2 Timothy 4:13

About What You Need to Learn

Think soberly about what you need to learn. We must develop ourselves. To do something with excellence we need to continue to learn. One area we would do well to focus upon is what we read. Clearly, books were important to Paul. What kinds of books should we read? Oswald Chambers suggested we choose books for their spiritual benefit, and those that would stimulate intellectual growth and help cultivate preaching style. He also suggested we not be content with easy books or satisfied with reading only in our specialty. A good technique is to read and reread books that were especially meaningful. Write on the inside of the back cover a brief analysis of the book to make a solid imprint on your memory. Oswald suggested we use reading to cut a channel between our reading and preaching.[128]

Breakout churches have an insatiable appetite to learn.[129] What we read and how we read is critically important. How quickly you get through reading material is immaterial. What is material is how much of the material gets through to you.[130] The key is that we are always learning and always striving to fulfill the ministry God has put before us.

About the Value of the Ministry

> *If I say, "I will not mention him, or speak any more in his name," there is in my heart as it were a burning fire shut up in my bones, and I am weary with holding it in, and I cannot.*
>
> Jeremiah 20:9

Take a sober look at the value of your ministry. The average Southern Baptist Church minister has been a senior pastor at 3.6 churches in his career, and 37 percent of SBC pastors have led four or more churches. Only Methodists exceed this—but Methodists usually are assigned positions by their denomination, and the average assignment lasts only about four years before the pastor is moved to another church by the denomination.[131] In Rainer's research, the average pastoral tenure was 3.6 years as well. However, studies showed that pastors who were most effective had tenures ranging from 11.2 to 21.6 years.[132]

I encourage you to strive for long pastoral tenures and to keep ministering. Even though we have setbacks, we cannot just walk away from the ministry. Consider the passage above from Jeremiah. You could paraphrase the passage to say, "If I were to say, 'I will no longer minister,' I would be miserable." Have you found that to be true as well? Research on pastors indicates that pastors who persevere in the ministry tend to feel more fulfilled. This is likely the result of feeling more and more competent as one adjusts to the challenges of life, and is also likely linked to learning the "ropes" of a particular church. If one leaves quickly into their tenure, they will fail to benefit from the inevitable competencies developed from working with people over time.

Further, even though pastors usually earn less money than their educational level might warrant in a secular position, most feel financially secure. Ninety-one percent of pastors are satisfied with their quality of life compared to 78 percent of practicing Christians and 62 percent of U.S. adults.[133] In one study, 89 percent of clergy were glad they entered the ministry, 88 percent believed their work had a positive influence on others, and 80 percent felt they had accomplished many worthwhile things in ministry.[134]

> *By the Holy Spirit who dwells within us, guard the good deposit entrusted to you.*
>
> 2 Timothy 1:14

So enjoy the ride. Rather than being sidetracked or succumbing to setbacks, remember you do what you do for the Lord. He is watching and He is pleased when you are focused upon Him and intend to honor Him. He walks beside you every step of the way and is helping you no matter what. As you minister, remember that so much of what Jesus did was for people like us who were born thousands of years after He served on the earth. Remember you, too, are often preparing the way for people who are not even at your church yet. You are part of something bigger than yourself, as the pastor quoted below indicated.[135]

> "We pastors need to know that we are part of something bigger than ourselves and that we, together, are called to a great destiny—we need leaders who are themselves passionate about the mission of our church and then personally, enthusiastically communicate that mission to us."

There is nothing like ministry. Ministry is rewarding in many ways. After the challenging situation with Ahab and Jezebel, Elijah mentored Elisha. He would never again say, "I alone follow God." He also became a different man. Rather than cowering in a cave and hiding from Jezebel, he went seeking Ahab (1 Kings 21). He found him and confronted him. Though he left this world (without dying) before Ahab and Jezebel met their demise, he was at peace, taking the long view and knowing he had done his part.

Ministry Is Rewarding in Many Ways

Ministry = Real Relationships
Ministry = Fulfilling Work
Ministry = Lasting Results

For me, the highlight of our year is our Christmas Eve service. All of the church members who are still in town come together as families to worship. At the end of the service I stand at the back of the church as the congregation sings a dismissal song. Often I look around the congregation and think of how God has helped so many of those there through the year that is coming to an end. I see people who have lost spouses, parents, and sometimes children. I see people who have been baptized, gotten married, had children, and simply become different people over time. I see my own family and think of how God has worked in their lives. It is so moving that sometimes I just want to cry. And then I tend to think, "There is nothing like ministry." There truly is not anything else that compares to ministry. My prayer for you wherever you may find yourself is that you will continue on ministering. Please do not quit. If you will persevere, you will reap in ways you have never imagined. Just do not lose heart.

And let us not grow weary of doing good, for in due season we will reap, if we do not give up.

Galatians 6:9

Endnotes

1 *The State of Pastors: How Today's Faith Leaders Are Navigating Life and Leadership in an Age of Complexity.* (2017). A Barna report produced in partnership with Pepperdine University.

2 E. Moody, & C. Royal. (2017). Pastoral Demands and Resilience Characteristics. *D6 Family Ministry Journal, 2:*17-28.

3 A. Berry, L. J. Francis, J. Rolph, & P. Rolph. (2012). Ministry and Stress: Listening to Anglican Clergy in Wales. *Pastoral Psychology, 61:*165-178.

C. Lee, & J. Iverson-Gilbert. (2003). Demand, Support, and Perception in Family-Related Stress Among Protestant Clergy. *Family Relations, 52*(3):249-257.

4 K. R. Meek, M. R. McMinn, C. M. Brower, T. D. Burnett, B. W. McRay, M. L. Ramey, D. W. Swanson, & D. D. Villa. (2003). Maintaining Personal Resiliency: Lessons Learned From Evangelical Protestant Clergy. *Journal of Psychology and Theology, 31*(4):339-347.

5 J. H. Morgan. (1999). *Scholar, Priest, and Pastor: Ministry Priorities Among Clergy Today.* Levering, MI: Wyndham Hall Press.

6 C. Doehring. (2013). New Directions for Clergy Experiencing Stress: Connecting Spirit and Body. *Pastoral Psychology, 62:*623-638.

G. W. Halaas. (2002). *Ministerial Health and Wellness. Evangelical Lutheran Church in America.* Chicago, IL: Evangelical Lutheran Church in America.

7 N. E. Q. Guzman, & L. A. Teh. (2016). Understanding the Stresses and Coping Resources of Filipino Clergy Families: A Multiple-Case Study. *Pastoral Psychology, 65:*459-480.

8 Ibid. p. 466.

9 A. Berry, et al. (2012).

C. Lee, & J. Iverson-Gilbert. (2003).

10 J. M. Faucett, R. F. Corwyn, & T. H. Poling. (2013). Clergy Role Stress: Interactive Effects of Role Ambiguity and Role Conflict on Intrinsic Job Satisfaction. *Pastoral Psychology, 62:*291-304.

L. K. Barnard, & J. F. Curry. (2012). The Relationship of Clergy Burnout to Self-Compassion and Other Personality Dimensions. *Pastoral Psychology, 61:*149-163.

11 N. E. Q. Guzman, & L. A. Teh. (2016). p. 468.

12 A. Berry, et al. (2012).

13 M. R. Mehl, C. L. Raison, T. W. W. Pace, J. M. G. Arevalo, & S. W. Cole. (2017). Natural Language Indicators of Differential Gene Regulation in the Human Immune System. *PNAS, 114*(47):12554-12559.

14 E. Pool, T. Brosch, S. Delplanque, & D. Sander. (2014). Stress Increases Cue-Triggered "Wanting" for Sweet Reward in Humans, *Journal of Experimental Psychology: Animal Learning and Cognition; 41*(2):128-36.

15 K. Zlatan, & G. Hisler. (2018) Sleepy Anger: Restricted Sleep Amplifies Angry Feelings. *Journal of Experimental Psychology: General.* DOI: 10.1037/xge0000522.

16 H. R. Jerajani, B. Jaju, M. M. Phiske, & N. Lade. (2009). Hematohidrosis: A Rare Clinical Phenomenon. *Indian Journal of Dermatology, 54:*290-292.

17 L. K. Barnard, & J. F. Curry. (2012).

G. L. Rediger. (1982). *Coping With Clergy Burnout.* Valley Forge, PA: Judson Press.

18 *The State of Pastors.* (2017).

L. K. Barnard, & J. F. Curry. (2012).

19 L. K. Barnard, & J. F. Curry. (2012).

20 B. A. Binau. (2006). Administrative Ministry: A Link Between Shame and Stress. *Trinity Seminary Review, 27*(2):99-106.

21 L. K. Barnard, & J. F. Curry. (2012).

22 Ibid..

23 J. M. Faucett, R. F. Corwyn, & T. H. Poling. (2013).

24 K. R. Meek, et al. (2003).

25 E. W. Mills, & J. P. Koval. (1971). *Stress in the Ministry*. Washington, DC: Ministry Studies Board.

26 K. R. Meek, et al. (2003).

27 *The State of Pastors*. (2017).

28 L. K. Barnard, & J. F. Curry. (2012).

29 K. R. Meek, et al. (2003).

30 J. Bridges. (1996). *Maintaining a Heart Yielded to God*. In H.B. London, *Refresh, Renew, Revive*. Colorado Springs, CO: Focus on the Family.

31 *The State of Pastors*. (2017).

32 Ibid.

33 K. R. Meek, et al. (2003).

34 Ibid.

35 Ibid.

36 N. E. Q. Guzman, & L. A. Teh. (2016). p. 469.

37 Ibid.

38 Ibid.

39 *The State of Pastors*. (2017).

40 Baptist Press. (2001). *Poll: Many Pastors Feel Lonely and Discouraged*. Accessed on January 1, 2019 at: http://www.bpnews.net/36377/poll-many-pastors-feel-lonely-discouraged.

41 *The State of Pastors*. (2017).

42 J. Oswald Chambers. (1967). *Spiritual Leadership: Principles of Excellence for Every Believer*. Chicago, IL: Moody Publishers.

43 Ambrose, S. E. (1992). *Band of Brothers: E Company, 506th Regiment, 101st Airborne: From Normandy to Hitler's Eagle's Nest*. New York, NY: Simon & Schuster.

44 E. Stetzer, & M. Dodson. (2007). *Comeback Churches: How 300 Churches Turned Around and Yours Can Too*. Nashville, TN: B & H Publishing Group.

45 S. Sonnentag, & C. Fritz. (2015). Recovery From Job Stress: The Stressor Detachment Model as an Integrative Framework. *Journal of Organizational Behavior, 36*:S72-S103.

46 S. Sonnentag. (2012). Psychological Detachment From Work During Leisure Time: The Benefits of Mentally Disengaging From Work. *Current Directions in Psychological Science, 21*(2):114–118.

47 L. K. Barnard, & J. F. Curry. (2012).

48 S. Sonnentag. (2012).

49 J. de Bloom, M. Kompier, S. Geurts, C. de Weerth, T. Taris, & S. Sonnentag. (2009). Do We Recover From Vacation? Meta-analysis of Vacation Effects on Health and Well-Being. *Journal of Organizational Behavior, 51*(1):13-25.

50 K. Weir. (2019). Give Me a Break: Psychologists Explore the Type and Frequency of Breaks We Need to Refuel Our Energy and Enhance Our Well-Being. *Monitor on Psychology, 50*(1):40-46.

51 A. Rees, M. W. Wiggins, W. S. Helton, T. Loveday, D. O'Hare. (2017). The Impact of Breaks on Sustained Attention in a Simulated, Semi-Automated Train Control Task. *Journal of Applied Cognitive Psychology, 31*(3):351-359.

52 H. H. Sievertsen, F. Gino, & M. Piovesan. (2016). Cognitive Fatigue Influences Students' Performance on Standardized Tests. *Proceedings of the National Academy of Sciences, 113*(10):2621-2624.

53 A. Rees, et al. (2017).

54 M. Sianoja, C. J. Syrek, J. de Bloom, K. Korpela, & U. Kinnunen. (2018). Enhancing Daily Well-Being at Work Through Lunchtime Park Walks and Relaxation Exercises: Recovery Experiences as Mediators. *Journal of Occupational Health Psychology, 23*(3):428-442.

55 E. M. Hunter, & C. Wu. (2016). Give Me a Better Break: Choosing Workday Break Activities to Maximize Resource Recovery. *Journal of Applied Psychology, 101*(2):302-311.

56 S. Toker, & M. Biron. (2012). Job Burnout and Depression: Unraveling Their Temporal Relationship and Considering the Role of Physical Activity. *Journal of Applied Psychology, 97*(3):699-710.

57 L. Xie, H. Kang, Q. Xu, M. J. Chen, Y. Liao, M. Thiyagarajan, J. O'Donnell, D. J. Christensen, C. Nicholson, J. J. Iliff, T. Takano, R. Deane, & M. Nedergaard. (2013). Sleep Drives Metabolite Clearance From the Adult Brain, *Science, 18:*373-377.

58 R. J. Proeschold-Bell, & S. H. LeGrand. (2012). High Rates of Obesity and Chronic Disease Among United Methodist Clergy. *Obesity, 18*(9):1867-1870.

59 G. W. Halaas. (2002).

60 Christianity Today Gleanings. (March 2015). Accessed on January 5, 2019 at https://www.christianitytoday.com/ct/2015/march/gleanings-march-2015.html.

61 M. R. Mehl, et al. (2017).

Centers for Disease Control and Prevention. (2008). *Road to Health Activities Guide*. Atlanta, GA: U.S. Department of Health and Human Services, Centers for Disease Control and Prevention.

62 D. Suchet: In the Footsteps of Saint Paul. *BBC One*. Accessed on January 5, 2019 at https://www.bbc.co.uk/programmes/b01pq9h5.

63 C. A. Demsky, C. Fritz, L. B. Hammer, & A. E. Black. (2018). Workplace Incivility and Employee Sleep: The Role of Rumination and Recovery Experiences. *Journal of Occupational Health Psychology*. Advance online publication. http://dx.doi.org/10.1037/ocp0000116.

64 P. D. Tomporowski. (20030. Effects of Acute Bouts of Exercise on Cognition. *Acta Psychologica, 112:*297-324.

M. Oppezzo, & D. L. Schwartz. (2014). Give Your Ideas Some Legs: The Positive Effect of Walking on Creative Thinking. *Journal of Experimental Psychology, 40:*1142-1152.

65 M. Niedermeier, J. Einwanger, A. Hartl, & M. Kopp. (2017). Affective Responses in Mountain Hiking—A Randomized Crossover Trial Focusing on Differences Between Indoor and Outdoor Activity. *PLoS ONE 12*(5).

66 R. J. Bretland, & E. B. Thorsteinsson. (2015). Reducing Workplace Burnout: The Relative Benefits of Cardiovascular and Resistance Exercise. *PeerJ—The Journal of Life and Environmental Sciences, 3:e89*. https://doi.org/10.7717/peerj.891.

67 S. J. H. Biddle, K. Fox, & S. Boutcher. (2003). *Physical Activity and Psychological Well-Being.* London, UK: Routledge.

68 J. M. Faucett, R. F. Corwyn, & T. H. Poling. (2013).

69 J. Bridges. (1996).

70 Baptist Press. (2011).

71 N. E. Q. Guzman, & L. A. Teh. (2016). p. 468.

72 C. Doehring. (2013).

73 D. Merrill. (1985). *Clergy Couples in Crisis: The Impact of Stress on Pastoral Marriages.* Waco, TX: Word Books. p. 16.

74 N. E. Q. Guzman, & L. A. Teh. (2016). p. 467.

75 Ibid. p. 467-468.

76 J. M. Faucett, R. F. Corwyn, & T. H. Poling. (2013).

77 N. E. Q. Guzman, & L. A. Teh. (2016). p. 468.

78 Ibid. p. 468.

79 J. S. House. (1981). *Work Stress and Social Support.* Reading, MA: Addison-Wesley.
C. R. Well. (2013). The Moderating Effects of Congregational and Denominational Support on the Impact of Stress on Clerical Emotional and Physical Health Status. *Pastoral Psychology, 62*:873-888.

80 Z. W. Adams, J. C. Sieverdes, B. Brunner-Jackson, M. Mueller, J. Chandler, V. Diaz, S. Patel, L. R. Sox, S. Wilder, & F. A. Treiber. (2018). Meditation smartphone application effects on prehypertensive adults' blood pressure: Dose-response feasibility trial. *Health Psychology, 37*(9):850-860.

81 J. S. House. (1981).
C. R. Well. (2013).

82 Baptist Press. (2011).

83 G. L. Rediger. (1982).

84 A. C. Maher, S. Kielb, E. Loyer, M. Connelley, A. Rademaker, M. M. Mesulam, S. Weintraub, D. McAdams, R. Logan, & E. Rogalski. (2017). Psychological Well-Being in Elderly Adults With Extraordinary Episodic Memory. *PLoS ONE, 12*(10). https://journals.plos.org/plosone/article?id=10.1371/journal.pone.0186413.

85 J. P. Gouin, B. Zhou, & S. Fitzpatrick. (2015). Social Integration Prospectively Predicts Changes in Heart Rate Variability Among Individuals Undergoing Migration Stress. *Annals of Behavioral Medicine, 49*(2):230.

86 *The State of Pastors.* (2017).

87 C. Lee, & J. Iverson-Gilbert. (2003).

88 L. K. Barnard, & J. F. Curry. (2012).

89 K. R. Meek, et al. (2003).

90 R. A. Clay. (2018). Are you Burned Out? Here Are the Signs and What to Do About Them. *Monitor on Psychology, 49*(2):31-34.

91 T. Rainer. (2005). *Breakout Churches.* Grand Rapids, MI: Zondervan.

92 E. Moody, & C. Royal. (2017).

93 Baptist Press. (2011).

94 E. Moody, & C. Royal. (2017).

95 *The State of Pastors.* (2017).

96 T. S. Rainer. (2005). p. 45.

97 *The State of Pastors.* (2017).

98 Ibid.

99 A. Malphurs, & G. E. Penfold. (2014). *Re:Vision: The Key to Transforming Your Church.* Grand Rapids, MI: Baker Books.

100 L. K. Barnard, & J. F. Curry. (2012). The Relationship of Clergy Burnout to Self-Compassion and Other Personality Dimensions. *Pastoral Psychology, 61*:149-163.

A. Berry, et al. (2013).

101 A. Malphurs, & G. E. Penfold. (2014).

102 G. P. Jackson. (January/February 2019). *The 7 People Christians Trust More Than Their Pastors.* Accessed at https://www.christianitytoday.com/news/2019/january/gallup-pastor-clergy-trust-professions-poll.html.

M. Brenan. (December 20, 2018). *Gallup.* Nurses Again Outpace Other Professions for Honesty, Ethics. Accessed at https://news.gallup.com/poll/245597/nurses-again-outpace-professions-honesty-ethics.aspx?utm_source=alert&utm_medium=email&utm_content=morelink&utm_

campaign=syndication.

103 *The State of Pastors.* (2017).

104 L. W. Farris. (July/August 2008). Centered in God, Centered in Time: Pastoral Leadership in Times of Change. *The Clergy Journal.* p. 6-8.

105 *The State of Pastors.* (2017).

106 Ibid.

107 R. J. Proeschold-Bell, & S. H. LeGrand. (2012).

108 J. Floyd. (2010). *Ten Things Every Minister's Wife Needs to Know.* Green Forest, AR: New Leaf Press.

109 J. Floyd. (2016). Woman to Woman-For the Pastor's Wife. *SBC Life.* p. 24.

110 G. L. Rediger. (1997). *Clergy Killers: Guidance for Pastors and Congregations Under Attack.* Louisville, KY: Westminster John Know Press.

111 Ibid.

112 Ibid.

113 L. Cameron. (1999). Specifying Intrusive Demands and Their Outcomes in Congregational Ministry: A Report on the Ministry Demands Inventory. *Journal for the Scientific Study of Religion, 38*(4):477-489.

114 D. McCullough. (1972, 2001). *The Great Bridge: The Epic Story of the Building of the Brooklyn Bridge.* New York, NY: Simon & Schuster.

115 N. E. Q. Guzman, & L. A. Teh. (2016). p. 468-469.

116 S. B. Leas. *The Clergy Killer Debate.* Accessed at https://alban.org/archive/the-clergy-killer-debate/ on February 1, 2019.

117 *The State of Pastors.* (2017).

118 T. G. Bandy. (2016). *Spiritual Leadership: Why Leaders Lead and Who Seekers Follow.* Nashville, TN: Abingdon Press.

119 T. Rainer. (2005).

120 B. A. Binau. (2006).

121 T. Rainer. (2005).

122 S. A. Golder, & M. W. Macy. (2011). Diurnal and Seasonal Mood Vary With Work, Sleep, and Daylength Across Diverse Cultures. *Science, 30:*1878-1881.

123 J. Chen, E. Demers, & L. Baruch. (2018). Oh What a Beautiful Morning! Diurnal Influences on Executives and Analysts: Evidence From Conference Calls. Management Science. *Home Management Science, 64*(12).

[124] K. Weir. (June 2018). Good Timing: When Is the Best Time to Take a Rest or Take a Test or Think Creatively? *Monitor on Psychology*.

[125] *The State of Pastors*. (2017).

[126] J. M. Faucett, R. F. Corwyn, & T. H. Poling. (2013).

[127] T. Rainer. (2005).

[128] J. Oswald Chambers. (1967).

[129] T. Rainer. (2005).

[130] J. Oswald Chambers. (1967).

[131] R. Sellers. (September/October 2005). "Pastors Think Pastors Should Stay Put." *Facts & Trends, 51*(5):4-5.

[132] T. Rainer. (2005).

[133] *The State of Pastors*. (2017).

[134] L. J. Francis, P. Kaldor, M. Robbins, & K. Castle. (2005). Happy but Exhausted? Work-Related Psychological Health Among Clergy. *Pastoral Sciences, 24:*101-120.

C. Doehring. (2013).

[135] K. R. Meek, et al. (2003).

Also Available by Edward E. Moody

Surviving Culture Parent Edition

When Character and Your World Collide

by Edward E. Moody

Paperback

ISBN 13: 9780892659838

$9.99

Surviving Culture

When Character and Your World Collide

by Edward E. Moody

Paperback

ISBN 13: 9780892656875

$9.99

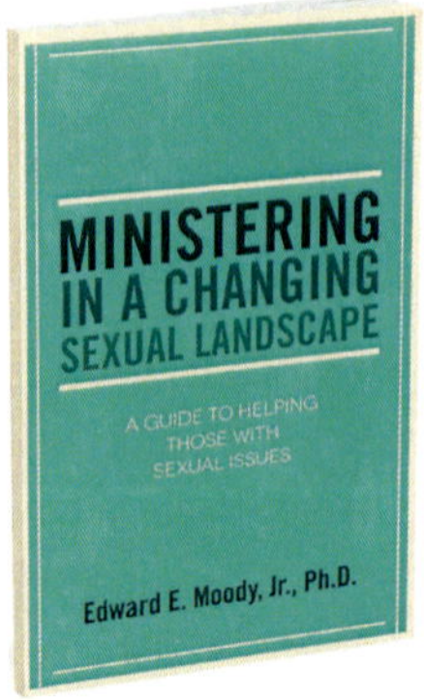

Ministering in a Changing Sexual Landscape

A Guide to Helping Those With Sexual Issues

by Dr. Edward E. Moody, Jr.

Paperback

ISBN 13: 9780892659869

$8.99

www.D6family.com

1-800-877-7030